REVIEW OF HEALTH AND SOCIAL SERVICES FOR MENTALLY DISORDERED OFFENDERS AND OTHERS REQUIRING SIMILAR SERVICES

Chairman: Dr John Reed

FINAL SUMMARY REPORT

Presented to Parliament
by the Secretary of State for Health
and the Home Department
by Command of Her Majesty

November 1992

Cm 2088

LONDON: HMSO
£12·40 net

CONTENTS

Richmond House

79 Whitehall

London SW1A 2NS

HOME OFFICE

QUEEN ANNE'S GATE

LONDON SW1H 9AT

Parliamentary Under

Secretary of State

FOREWORD

We are grateful to Dr John Reed, his Steering Committee colleagues and all those who have contributed in other ways to this joint review of health and social services for mentally disordered offenders and others with similar needs. One immediate effect of this work, combined with other recent developments, has been to raise awareness of this group of patients to probably the highest level since Lord Butler's Committee reported in 1975.

The Government has reaffirmed in the course of the review that, wherever possible, mentally disordered offenders should receive care and treatment from health and social services, rather than the criminal justice system. We have also endorsed a statement of guiding principles pointing, consistently with the need to ensure public safety, to a more local and less institutional pattern of services for the majority of patients. This calls not only for a flexible range of services to be available to assess and meet indivudual needs, but for the various agencies in both the statutory and non-statutory sectors to work together to similar ends.

The people with whom this review is concerned occupy a sensitive poisition at the meeting point of the health and social services and the criminal justice system. The work of the review complements action taken by the Government to develop mental health services more generally through initiatives such as the care programme approach. Mental illness is also one of the five key areas selected in the White Paper, *The Health of the Nation,* with the special needs of mentally disordered offenders as a specific priority.

In some areas significant progress has been made already. Following the Home Office circular 66/90 which preceded the review, a number of court diversion and similar schemes have been established through locally resourced initiatives. Several local multi-agency schemes are being "pump-primed" through contributions from central Government. Regional Directors of Public Health have undertaken initial assessments of needs in their regions and these will be further developed in the light of experience. Meanwhile provision of medium secure units is being enhanced by a sixfold increase in central Government capital funding in 1992-93.

This final summary report contains some 276 recommendations. Many are about good practice and good co-operation between agencies. Others relate to proposed service developments which, as the report makes clear, cannot be achieved overnight. We shall be considering the advice in this report and the earlier consultative reports, whose general direction has been widely supported. We are also publishing, for consultation, a report on services for offenders with learning disabilities or with autism and a discussion paper on racial and cultural issues. Our Departments will welcome comments on those documents and, indeed, any further views on the issues discussed in the final report. In addition we have set up two further working groups (also under Dr Reed's chairmanship) to consider high security psychiatric services and those for people with psychopathic disorder. These will be reporting in the early part of 1993.

In order to maintain a focus for the agencies concerned at national level we are establishing a new advisory committee on mentally disordered offenders. This will be formed for a period of three years with the job of advising our Departments on matters concerned with the provision and coordiation of services, including, in particular, the follow-up to the review.

We shall be making decisions in due course about which of the review's recommendations we can accept and the pace at which it will be possible to implement them, bearing in mind the resources available. A positive start has been made. We shall work together to build on that foundation.

TIM YEO
Parliamentary Secretary
Department of Health

MICHAEL JACK
Minister of State
Home Office

November 1992

OTHER DOCUMENTS PRODUCED BY THE REVIEW

References in this report are by means of the abbreviation shown

AD REPORT OF THE ACADEMIC DEVELOPMENT ADVISORY GROUP (published for consultation in June 1992)

CR REPORT OF THE COMMUNITY ADVISORY GROUP (November 1991)

FN REPORT OF THE FINANCE ADVISORY GROUP (June 1992)

HR REPORT OF THE HOSPITAL ADVISORY GROUP (November 1991)

LD OFFICIAL WORKING GROUP ON SERVICES FOR PEOPLE WITH SPECIAL NEEDS: PEOPLE WITH LEARNING DISABILITIES OR WITH AUTISM (November 1992)

OV THE SERVICE ADVISORY GROUPS: AN OVERVIEW BY THE STEERING COMMITTEE (November 1991)

PR REPORT OF THE PRISON ADVISORY GROUP (November 1991)

RS REPORT OF THE RESEARCH ADVISORY GROUP (June 1992)

SN REPORT OF THE OFFICIAL WORKING GROUP ON SERVICES FOR PEOPLE WITH SPECIAL NEEDS (June 1992)

ST REPORT OF THE STAFFING AND TRAINING ADVISORY GROUP (June 1992)

SERVICES FOR PEOPLE FROM BLACK AND ETHNIC MINORITY GROUPS—ISSUES OF RACE AND CULTURE: A DISCUSSION PAPER (November 1992)

The earlier reports will be published by HMSO in four additional volumes:

Volume 2: Service needs (community, hospital and prison reports and Steering Committee *Overview*)

Volume 3: Finance, staffing and training (finance and staffing and training reports)

Volume 4: The academic and research base (academic development and research reports)

Volume 5: Special issues and differing needs (special needs report)

The report on learning disabilities and the discussion paper on racial and cultural issues are being published for consultation by the Department of Health and the Home Office.

1

THE REVIEW

1.1. This is the final report of the Steering Committee of the review of health and social services for mentally disordered offenders.

1.2. It summarises the principal issues emerging from the review. It does *not* supersede the earlier advisory group reports which contain detailed analysis of the many topics addressed over the past 18 months.

The Steering Committee and its terms of reference

1.3. The review was established by Department of Health and Home Office Ministers on 30 November under the chairmanship of Dr John Reed. We were appointed on 20 December 1990: see *Annex A*. We met for the first time on 31 January 1991 and completed our work on 23 July 1992.

1.4. Our terms of reference were:

> To plan, co-ordinate and direct a review of the health and social services provided in England by the NHS, Special Hospitals Service Authority and local authorities for mentally disordered offenders (and others requiring similar services) without having come before the courts, with a view to determining whether changes are needed in the current level, pattern, or operation of services and identifying ways of promoting such changes, having regard to:
>
> > the development of new management arrangements in the NHS and the proposals for the development of community care;
> >
> > the implications for NHS forensic psychiatry of action to follow up the report of the Home Office Efficiency Scrutiny on the Prison Medical Service;
> >
> > any relevant recommendations of the inquiry into the Strangeways (Manchester) prison disturbances (the Woolf Inquiry) and other prison-related inquiries;
>
> and including consideration of:
>
> > present arrangements for funding services and service developments, and their possible improvement;
> >
> > relevant research and studies;
>
> to produce regular reports to the Department of Health and the Home Office on the progress of the review and its findings, together with its recommendations.
>
> The review will be essentially concerned with assessing how services should be developed within the framework of existing legislation. It is not intended as a review of the law. However, the Steering Committee may propose amendments to the law if it considers that they would materially further the longer-term objectives of the review.

1.5. The review has been serviced jointly by officials of the sponsoring Departments. We should like to express our thanks to all the officials working on the review for their dedication and hard work.

Advisory and working groups

1.6. Much of our work was conducted through a series of advisory groups which comprised both Steering Committee and co-opted members.

1.7. Three initial groups looked at services provided:

> *in the community;*
> *in hospital; and*
> *in prison.*

1.8. Their reports were published for widespread consultation on 13 November 1991, together with an *Overview* of our own: see *Annex B*. We received some 200 responses which overwhelmingly supported the direction set out in the reports and made many other helpful comments.

1.9. A second tranche of advisory groups carried forward the framework established by the first and looked in particular at the resource implications of the earlier proposals. They were concerned with:

> *finance;*
> *staffing and training;*
> *research; and*
> *academic development.*

1.10. The reports of these groups were published for consultation on 2 June 1992, together with that of a working group of officials on *services for mentally disordered offenders with "special needs"* (see paragraph 3.7): see *Annex C*. Comments were requested by 1 September 1992. We have taken account of those received before the review ended.

1.11. The special needs group submitted to us on 23 July 1992 a report on *learning disabilities* (mental handicap) and *autism* (see paragraph 3.10), which is also being published.

1.12. The report of a working group on *performance management* was included in the report of the finance advisory group (FN, Annex F and paragraphs 8.17-19 below).

1.13. We have considered in detail a number of *racial and cultural issues:* see paragraphs 3.5-6. A discussion paper on these is being published.

Recommendations

1.14. Between them, the advisory and working groups made 270 recommendations, which we have endorsed. They are set out in full in Chapter 11. We have made six further recommendations to supplement the earlier ones.

1.15. The most fundamental recommendations are considered as part of the proposed "way forward" in Chapter 10.

Wales, Scotland and Northern Ireland

1.16. Our remit extended only to England, but our work has some implications for services in other parts of the United Kingdom, in particular for staffing and training and, in the case of Wales, for secure provision and some Home Office responsibilities. There have been regular liaison meetings between review officials and their territorial counterparts.

Wales

1.17. The *Report of the All-Wales Advisory Group on Forensic Psychiatry* was published for consultation in March 1992. The development of specialised services in the Principality (including its first medium secure unit recently opened at Bridgend) will have implications for services in England. In particular, some 70 Welsh patients with high security needs are provided for in English Special Hospitals and there are also admissions to medium secure units in England (*ibid,* paragraph 4.9). The Welsh report envisaged a continuing relationship with the Special Hospitals on a more co-ordinated basis (*ibid,* paragraphs 7.21-22).

1.18. There may need to be further discussions between the Department of Health, the Home Office and the Welsh Office about the specific implications of the respective reviews.

Visits

1.19. Review officials and Steering Committee members have taken part in a number of field visits. These have enabled several hundred people involved in various ways with mentally disordered offenders to contribute to the review. Visits to every Health Region have provided a base for multi-agency discussions, as well as the opportunity to see health, social and criminal justice service in a range of settings. There have been other visits to voluntary and independent services and to Special Hospital facilities. Seminars in every Social Services Inspectorate region have been attended by representatives of virtually all social services departments; reports of these have been widely disseminated. There was also a visit to the Netherlands.

1.20. We are extremely grateful to all those who contributed to these visits and other discussions in the course of the review. Arrangements are being made to distribute an informal digest which highlights some of the key messages emerging from the visits and a number of local initiatives. The advisory group reports have taken account of other findings from the visits.

1.21. In the course of the review, a number of agencies have held conferences or other events of their own which have been designed to further the work of the review or otherwise to raise awareness of the needs of mentally disordered offenders. We very much welcome these initiatives which have helped to raise the profile of services in this difficult, complex, and all too often neglected area to a much higher level than for many years.

Working group on psychopathic disorder

1.22. The issues concerning the care and treatment of people with psychopathic (or personality) disorders are difficult and contentious. We have already given detailed consideration to these as a Committee, but Ministers have accepted our recommendation that they call for further, urgent work before it will be possible to offer any conclusions.

1.23. A joint Department of Health/Home Office advisory group with the following terms of reference will report by March 1993:

> To consider the services needed for those people who present special problems of violent behaviour or repeated offending because of their personality, whether or not they are otherwise mentally disordered, taking account of both the interests of the individuals concerned and the protection of other people, In particular:
>
> to consider, in the light of present knowledge, what methods of management or treatment are likely to be most effective in reducing violent or offending behaviour;
>
> to consider whether these require the provision of any new services in addition to or in place of those available at present;
>
> to advise how the services, whether within the prison service, the health service or elsewhere may most effectively be made available to those in need;
>
> to consider whether any changes are needed in the present legal provisions relating to psychopathic disorder in the interests of more effective provision of services;
>
> to advise on any research which might facilitate the better understanding of the definition, management or treatment of this group of offenders;
>
> to consider the resource implications of any proposals, including their cost-effectiveness.

THE INHERITANCE

2.1. It will be apparent from our terms of reference that the review has taken place in the wake of other important developments, including major changes in the management of the health and social services. We have had to address a number of pressing practical issues, but we have had in mind also the opportunity to make policy and service proposals which, if adopted, would influence the direction of services well into the next century.

A continuing story

2.2. By the late Middle Ages it had been established as lawful to imprison someone if he were mentally disordered "and you believed that he was going to do some mischief like burning down a house" (Allderidge, *Brit J Psychiat* (1979) 134, 326). The Vagrancy Act 1744 distinguished impoverished "lunatics" from "rogues, vagabonds, sturdy beggars and vagrants" and ordered the apprehension of those who were "furiously mad and dangerous ... in such secure place ... as justices shall ... direct and appoint" (see Donnelly (1983) *Managing the Mind*, Ch 11). From the early 19th century, legislation and service provision for "lunatics" and "criminal lunatics" developed along generally separate lines, though in both cases it was largely institutional or custodial. The first of what are now the Special Hospitals opened at Broadmoor in 1863.

2.3. The particular kind of problems we have been examining are not new. Almost 100 years ago, Thomas Holmes described "the ever increasing army of the demented" coming before magistrates' courts, the remanding of defendants to prison for medical reports, and the training needs of prison doctors (*Pictures and Problems from London Police Courts*, 1900). At about the same time (1897-8), Oscar Wilde was writing to the *Daily Chronicle* about his first-hand experience of conditions in Reading Gaol, including the plight of a young man "more than usually half-witted ... noticed by all the other prisoners on account of the strangeness of his conduct".

Percy (1957) and beyond

2.4. By the middle of this century, the Percy Commission (*Royal Commission on the Law Relating to Mental Illness and Mental Deficiency 1954-1957*, Cmnd 169) discerned that:

> public opinion in general is moving towards a more enlightened attitude, which is fostered by the progress which has been made during the last fifty years in the understanding and treatment of mental disorders (*ibid*, paragraph 68).

2.5. Percy pointed the way to a new emphasis on community care and to the breaking down of barriers between mentally ill and mentally handicapped people and the general population. This led to the Mental Health Act of 1959, which replaced a multitude of legislation on criminal lunacy and mental deficiency, much of it dating from the last century, and ultimately to two major White Papers in the 1970s, *Better Services for the Mentally Handicapped* (Cmnd 4683, 1971) and *Better Services for the Mentally Ill* (Cmnd 6233, 1975). The latter have set the broad direction for policy ever since.

Butler/Glancy (1974–75)

2.6. The specific needs of mentally disordered offenders were examined in 1972–75 by the Butler committee (*Report of the Committee on Mentally Abnormal Offenders* (1975), Cmnd 6244), which concluded that:

> The overriding need is to provide the best possible treatment for the patient's mental disorder and he should have full access to treatment in the best location that will suit his needs. Ultimately in individual cases this must depend on clinical judgment, but in general policy we hope that humane counsels will prevail, and that considerations of a patient's background will not be allowed to obscure that basic principle (*ibid*, paragraph 1.10; CR 4.27).

2.7. Butler recommended the provision of 2,000 places in secure hospital units below the levels of security obtaining in the Special Hospitals. In parallel, the Glancy working party (DHSS (1974) *Report of the Working Party on NHS Psychiatric Hospitals:* HR, Annex B), addressing the needs of only those already in hospital, proposed 1,000 such places. Between them, these recommendations gave rise to the medium (or Regional) secure unit programme which over the past 16 years has provided some 600 permanent beds, still a long way short of even the "Glancy" target (see paragraphs 5. 19–25).

Developments since 1975

2.8. Since the 1970s, forensic psychiatry has come to be seen as a specialty in its own right. There are now over 70 consultants, compared to just two 30 years ago (ST 4.6). A new Mental Health Act was passed in 1983. In 1987 a Department of Health/Home Office working group made recommendations for the smoother transfer of mentally disordered offenders from the prison system to the NHS. In 1989 the Special Hospitals Service Authority took over the management of high security psychiatric provision from the Department of Health.

2.9. All these developments, together with the growth of community-based services, had their positive effect on many patients. In the words of the community care White Paper, *Caring for People* (Cm 849, 1989):

> Where it is effectively implemented, the new style of service offers a much higher quality of life for people with a mental illness and a service more appreciated by their families than is possible in the traditional large and often remote mental hospital. The Government reaffirms its support of the policy as a civilised and humanitarian one (*ibid,* paragraph 7.4).

2.10. However, as the then Parliamentary Secretary for Health said of mentally disordered offenders when he announced this review in 1990:

> There remains great potential—and a great need for—further progress in this difficult area. Some mentally disordered offenders, for example, remain in unsuitable placements: people in prison who should be in hospital; others in maximum secure provision who need a less secure regime. There is undoubtedly under-provision of a suitable range of accommodation in certain areas...(Department of Health Press Release H90/581).

1990–1: a watershed?

2.11. 1990–1 may come to be seen in retrospect as marking a watershed in approaches to mentally disordered offenders. A number of major developments came together almost simultaneously.

2.12. In September 1990 the Home Office, supported by the Department of Health, issued its Circular 66/90 (NHS Management Executive Letter (90)168) (see **Annex D**) which promoted diversion and discontinuance mechanisms as means of ensuring that offenders do not get caught up needlessly in the criminal justice system. The Efficiency Scrutiny of the Prison Medical Service (1990) proposed that health care should be contracted in to prisons, predominantly from the NHS, and the Woolf report on disturbances at Manchester (Strangeways) Prison and elsewhere (Cm 1456, 1991) made far-reaching recommendations for the improvement of prison regimes. The Chief Inspector of Prisons brought into sharp focus concerns about suicide and self-harm among prisoners (*Report of a Review of Suicide and Self-Harm in Prison Establishments* (Cm 1383, 1990). Research (Gunn et al (1991) *Mentally disordered prisoners)* suggested that upwards of 700 sentenced prisoners might require transfer to psychiatric care in NHS hospitals (see paragraph 5.30); a study of the remand population was completed in July 1991 (see paragraphs 5.3 and 5.30).

Protection of services: Executive Letters (90)190 and (92)6

2.13. The National Health Service and Community Care Act 1990 delineated more closely responsibilities for the provision of health and social care and introduced to the NHS from April 1991 "purchaser/provider" arrangements. New arrangements for local authorities apply from April 1993.

2.14. To ensure that health services for mentally disordered offenders and similar patients were sustained amid these changes, Regional General Managers were required to ensure their maintenance at least at April 1991 levels (NHS Management Executive Letter (90)190). On our recommendation (CR 4.18; OV 32), the effect of this instruction has been extended until 31 March 1993 "to ensure a stable base from which to develop services...following the current review" (EL(92)6): see Annex B.

"A strong lead"

2.15. Ministers were "determined to give a strong lead in these matters" (Press Release H90/581). Hence, this review. What follows are our findings and proposals for the future.

3

THE APPROACH WE HAVE TAKEN

3.1. The Government's long-standing policy has been that mentally disordered offenders needing care and treatment should receive it from the health and personal social services rather than in custodial care. We support that policy and welcome its reaffirmation by the Government (House of Commons written answer, 13 November 1991). However, we recognise that practice all too often falls a long way short of what is desirable (OV 14).

3.2. How to meet the shortfalls in both practice and provision has been at the heart of the review. Our attention has been directed in particular to:

    i. the level and range of provision that needs to be in place to enable mentally disordered offenders and similar patients to receive care and treatment in the most suitable location;

    ii. the mechanisms that will:

        a. estimate the numbers needing specialised services;

        b. identify and assess the needs of those who should be diverted before entry into the criminal justice system or as soon as possible thereafter;

        c. ensure effective joint working between the range of agencies locally (a process already strongly promoted by Home Office Circular 66/90) and Government departments nationally; and

        d. make the best use of available resources and ensure that there are no disincentives or unnecessary obstacles to providing the most effective care.

Guiding principles

3.3. We proposed a set of guiding principles for service provision (OV 16) which Ministers have endorsed (written answer, 13 Nov 1992). These are that patients should be cared for:

    i. *with regard to the quality of care and proper attention to the needs of individuals;*

    ii. *as far as possible, in the community, rather than in institutional settings;*

    iii. *under conditions of no greater security than is justified by the degree of danger they present to themselves or to others;*

    iv. *in such a way as to maximise rehabilitation and their chances of sustaining an independent life;*

    v. *as near as possible to their own homes or families if they have them.*

The needs of individuals and groups

3.4. This emphasis on individual needs calls for a positive approach to ensuring that all patients, whatever their background, receive the level and type of care that they require.

Race and culture

3.5. This is especially important for people from ethnic minority groups, in particular Afro-Caribbeans, who, relative to the general population, are over-represented among prisoners and are, for example, more likely than white people to be brought within the scope of the Mental Health Act 1983 or to be detained in a Special Hospital. In their case, particular account must be taken of social and cultural factors.

3.6. As noted at paragraph 1.13, issues of race and culture are considered in a detailed discussion paper: see *inset* and paragraphs 11.138-146.

ISSUES OF RACE AND CULTURE:

RECOMMENDATIONS FROM THE DISCUSSION PAPER

There should be strong proactive equal opportunity policies relating to race and culture established in all agencies involved with mentally disordered offenders. The policies should be known and understood by staff and made widely available. Implementation should be monitored.

There should be explicit consideration of race and culture in the professional and vocational training of all those working with mentally disordered offenders.

Early training on a multi-agency basis and linked to service provision should take place with the involvement of ethnic minority groups.

Organisations involved with services for mentally disordered offenders should review their strategies and policies in the light of issues of race and culture.

Health and local authorities should enable agencies from black and ethnic minority communities to develop and provide services for mentally disordered offenders.

Ethnic minority communities should be involved in the planning, development and monitoring of services for mentally disordered offenders.

Funding should be made available to establish an action research project on the diversion from custody of people from ethnic minority communities.

Research priorities should be discussed with members of the various ethnic minority communities and consideration given to their areas of concern.

A co-ordinated system of ethnicity data collection should be established within all agencies concerned with mentally disordered offenders.

Discussion papers on special or differing needs

3.7. The needs of a number of other people also present special issues by virtue of their condition, age or gender. In addition to a report on *learning disabilities* (see paragraph 3.10), the special needs working group produced a series of discussion papers (summarised at *Annex E*) which address the various issues in detail:

> *people with brain injury* (SN, Paper 1);
>
> *people who are deaf or hearing impaired* (SN, Paper 2);
>
> *drug and alcohol misusers* (SN, Paper 3);
>
> *sex offenders with mental health care needs* (SN, Paper 4);
>
> *potential suicides* (SN, Paper 5, and paragraph 8.19 below);
>
> *children and adolescents* (SN, Discussion Paper 6; LD 5.1-30);
>
> *elderly people* (SN, Paper 7); and
>
> *women* (SN, Paper 8).

3.8. A note on action to tackle the needs of *homeless mentally disordered offenders* is at *Annex F*. The need for further work on *psychopathic disorder* was identified at paragraphs 1.22-23 above.

Key requirements

3.9. In approaching these special issues, the following key requirements should apply (SN 2.2):

> i.   *that agencies adopt a positive and non-prejudicial approach, at both planning and operational level, to identifying and meeting special needs;*
>
> ii. *that effective links are maintained between general mental health, specialised forensic, criminal justice and other relevant services (learning disabilities, drugs and alcohol, etc);*
>
> iii. *that service provision is tailored to individual needs (paragraph 3.3 above);*
>
> iv. *that, in individual cases, the balance struck between the contribution of the various services is in the best interests of the patient (for example, in the case of children and adolescents, by weighing the respective mental health and child care requirements).*

People with learning disabilities (mental handicap) or autism

3.10. Only a very small minority of people with learning disabilities offend. Most have mild or "borderline" disabilities (LD 6.10-13). Their needs are often overlooked or go unidentified. Many of the general considerations advanced during this review apply equally to this group, but their requirements must have a special focus, including effective links with local learning disability services, including education, and access, where necessary, to specialised services. The issues, including those for offenders with *autism*, are considered in detail in the special needs working group report, *People with Learning Disabilities or with Autism*.

3.11. We have kept in touch with the project group, led by Professor Jim Mansell, that has been looking at services for *people with learning disabilities and severe psychiatric or behavioural disturbance*. This group has recently reported to the Department of Health.

4

THE FRAMEWORK

4.1. Mentally disordered offenders have widely differing needs. Some require specialised services because of their offending behaviour or other special needs, but the majority can be looked after within general mental health or learning disability services. The multi-agency planning and resourcing of these general services must take proper account of the needs of offender patients, in particular the need to cater for their diversion from the criminal justice system at the earliest opportunity (OV 17).

4.2. *General practitioners* see as many as 1 in 4 of the general population each year for some form of mental distress (*The Health of the Nation* (Cm 1523), 1991; CR 3.43; ST 2.14-16) and often have a pivotal role in the care of mentally disordered offenders.

4.3. The guiding principles at paragraph 3.3 imply an increased emphasis on community care, but it is equally clear that the range of hospital provision, in particular that in conditions of low to medium security, is inadequate overall to meet existing and projected need.

4.4. We emphasise also that diversion and service provision are parts of the same equation. There is little point in "diverting" someone if he or she has nowhere to go or if the placement is unsuitable or inadequate. This may simply lead to a deterioration, with the risk of further offending or resort to crisis intervention: the so-called *"revolving door" syndrome*. It may also be a poor use of resources.

Needs assessment

4.5. Information on the current level of services is limited and mainly confined to specialised or secure provision. This is because most offenders are (quite properly) numbered among those in mainstream services. Others are in the wrong place (for example, in prison when they need a secure hospital place, in a hospital with higher security than their treatment requires, or in hospital when they should be in the community). Information on the extent of unsuitable placements is not routinely available.

4.6. The starting point for determining future service patterns must be regular needs assessments, conducted on a multi-agency basis (HR 5.10; CR 4.2-10; ST 1.9-10):

> The agenda for future needs assessment . . . is precisely about defining the nature and level of services required to care for and improve the health of a population (NHS Management Executive (1991) *Assessing health care needs;* CR, Annex G).

> Health Authorities have the responsibility to identify the health needs of a geographically designated population and to ensure that appropriate action is taken to meet them. Social Services Departments have an equivalent responsibility to meet the social needs of such people. Reference to a base population specifies the responsibility of each Authority and makes it possible, through repeated epidemiologically-based assessments, to determine whether the duty is carried out (Wing (1992) *Epidemiologically-Based Mental Health Needs Assessments: Review of Research on Psychiatric Disorders (ICD-10, F2-F6)).*

> In their plans [social services departments] should identify the care needs of the local population taking into account factors such as age distribution, problems associated with living in inner city areas, special needs of ethnic minority communities, the number of homeless or transient people likely to require care (HMSO (1990) *Community Care in the Next Decade and Beyond,* paragraph 2.25).

> In order to assist with needs assessment . . . information about mentally disordered offenders in prisons and Special Hospitals should be regularly disseminated to each Regional Health Authority. This information should consist of [the] identity, location and health region of residence of prisoners who, in the opinion of the [Health Care Service for Prisoners] should be transferred to hospital under mental health legislation [and of] Special Hospital patients who, in the opinion of the Special Hospitals Service Authority, should be transferred to more local hospitals (HR 5.14-15).

4.7. In April 1992 Regional Directors of Public Health were asked to conduct, in conjunction with other agencies, an initial needs assessment for services for mentally disordered offenders and similar patients (including those with "special needs" such as learning disabilities or psychopathic disorder): NHS Management Executive Letter (92)24 (see *Annex G*). This assessment was concerned mainly with secure provision (see paragraphs 5.16-25), but was only a starting point. The exercise should be broadened to cover a wider range of services and repeated, in the light of experience and with necessary adaptations, in future years.

Multi-agency working

4.8. Effective multi-agency and multi-professional working is indispensable for services with so many diverse components. We are glad that Ministers have accepted the need for improved arrangements at both planning and operational level in this complex area (House of Commons written answer, 13 Nov 1991).

4.9. We have not been prescriptive about how we see agencies working together, nor which (if any) should take the lead. Local conditions, as well as agency boundaries, vary considerably (CR 3.24). The report of the community advisory group described a range of district, supra-district and Regional options (CR3.24-32). These would need to take account of the pattern and responsibilities of all agencies at Regional or sub-Regional level, as well as the realistic levels at which *purchaser or provider functions* could best be exercised (see paragraph 8.2-7), and the need to relate to the new *area committees for the criminal justice system* which are being established in the light of the Woolf report *(op cit,* paragraph 1.172; *Custody, Care and Justice* (Cm 1647 (1991), paragraphs 1.13-14). For the NHS specifically, we see an important and continuing Regional role (CR 3.29). Each Regional Health Authority must ensure that it has clearly identified sources of advice on services for mentally disordered offenders. This might include the appointment or designation of a *consultant in forensic psychiatry* "to advise the Regional Director of Public Health and with access to the Regional General Manager and Regional Health Authority" (HR 4.8 and Appendix 3).

Continuity of care

Multi-professional core teams

4.10. We envisage a multi-professional core team being responsible at local working level (possibly on a multi-district basis) for ensuring that mentally disordered offenders receive the care they need, usually from general mental health care or learning disability teams (CR 3.34-37; ST 5.8-12).

4.11. The membership of this will vary and not every potential contributor must see every patient. There may be some cross-membership with other client group teams; indeed, this may be helpful. The following groups will need to be involved in some way:

> *general practitioners* and other primary care workers (including dentists);
>
> *forensic and general psychiatrists*, and other medical staff such as psychotherapists, prison medical officers and forensic medical examiners (police surgeons);
>
> *nurses*, including community psychiatric nurses;
>
> *approved and generic social workers*, and other social services staff as necessary;
>
> *probation officers;*
>
> *clinical psychologists;*
>
> *occupational therapists, physiotherapists, speech therapists, other therapists* (art, drama, etc) and *interpreters;*
>
> *education staff.*

4.12. There should be links with the *police, prisons, courts, Crown Prosecution Service, voluntary and independent sectors* (see paragraphs 4.20-22), *the social security, housing and employment services,* and perhaps *local Law Societies* or an individual *solicitor* (ST 4.65; 5.11-12). Services for prisoners should increasingly become part of local mental health services (see paragraphs 5.29-33).

Information is an asset—when its available!

4.13. Working together effectively calls for better exchange of information, often across agency boundaries, and systematic tracking of casework. These requirements raise some ethical issues, with the need for safeguards, but, provided that these can be tackled without detriment to individual rights (as set out, for example, in the *Patients' Charter,* 1991), they are likely to be in the interests of patient care (ST 4.16-20; PR 4.13; National Unit for Psychiatric Research and Development (1988) *Towards Coordinated Care for People with Long-Term Severe Mental Illness*). We envisage that local multi-agency groups might have an important monitoring role in this area (ST 4.21).

Care programmes

4.14. Each person referred to the specialised mental health care services must have a "care programme" (CR 3.14-18; ST 5.30-34). This is mandatory for health and social services authorities under Health Circular (90)23/Local Authority Circular (90)11: see **Annex H.** The purpose of the care programme approach is:

> to seek to ensure that in future patients treated in the community receive the health and social care they need by:
>
> i.   introducing more systematic arrangements for deciding whether a patient referred to the specialised psychiatric services can, in the light of the available resources and the views of the patient and, where appropriate, his/her carers, realistically be treated in the community;
>
> ii. ensuring proper arrangements are made, and continue to be made, for the continuing health and social care for those patients who can be treated in the community (*ibid,* Annex, paragraph 4).

4.15. At present these arrangements do not apply as such to people with learning disabilities (SN 2.38-39), although the basic principles of the care programme approach represent good practice for all patients who come within the scope of this review (*Patients' Charter;* NHS Management Executive Letter (92)13/Chief Inspector Letter (92)10, Annex B; SN 2.32-33).

4.16. In the case of offenders, criminal justice staff need to be involved where necessary. We have recommended that the care programme guidance should be revised to make clear that the arrangements should apply specifically to:

i.   discharged prisoners with continuing mental health care needs (CR 3.16; PR 5.33-36; ST 5.30-33 and Annex O);

ii. offenders with learning disabilities leaving hospital or prison (SN 2.38-39). (Care programmes are already provided for mentally impaired and severely mentally impaired patients at Special Hospitals);

iii. mentally disordered offenders in non-statutory provision to whom the arrangements would apply if they were being cared for in the NHS (see paragraph 4.22); and

iv. patients remitted to prison after mental health treatment in hospital (ST 5.33).

Families, carers and users

4.17. There is an important role for patients, their families and other informal carers in planning services (CR 3.44-45). Patients should always be involved in the planning of their care programmes, as should families and carers whenever this is consistent with the patient's wishes. When a care programmme depends on a major contribution from family or other carers, this should be agreed with them in advance. Families and carers may also have needs of their own, including help in coping with particular stresses, including the practical effects of a family member being subject to a hospital order (for example, possibly lengthy travel to a Special Hospital to visit) or the unfair stigma that they themselves may attract as a result of the offence. Support for families at an early stage of mental distress may help to prevent deterioration and/or offending. Within the terms of the Children Act 1989, there may be particular implications for the welfare of any children.

Victims

4.18. Services must also be available to assist the victims of offences and their families. Indeed, offender and victim may be related. There may be particular considerations if an offender is mentally disordered: for example, the discontinuance of a prosecution or the imposition of a hospital order rather than a custodial sentence may lead the victim to feel that "punishment" is being evaded and the offence not being treated seriously. In some instances (eg some cases of sexual abuse), a victim may himself subsequently offend.

4.19. Victim support schemes have been set up in most areas. They have recommended to the Home Office that the police should be reminded to inform victims of the reasons why an offender is cautioned rather than prosecuted. Such advice is equally important if a mentally disordered offender is diverted from the criminal justice system or a medical disposal is likely. Volunteers working with support schemes may need training to help them support the victims of mentally disordered offenders.

★ **WE RECOMMEND that services dealing with mentally disordered offenders take account of the needs of victims and offer assistance and staff training where necessary.**

Links with voluntary, independent and "out-of-area" services

4.20. The voluntary, and independent sectors provide services for mentally disordered offenders. The contribution of the former is described in NACRO (1991) *The Resettlement of Mentally Disordered Offenders* (see *Annex I*) and that of independent hospitals at paragraph 5.28 below. There is a growing number of independent residential care and nursing homes, registered by local authorities, which admit people with a mental illness or learning disability.

4.21. We have made no general assumptions that particular services should be provided by statutory agencies. What is important is that non-statutory services are involved both in service planning and, as necessary, in care planning. An immediate concern is that the contribution of voluntary agencies to the care (and, in particular, the accommodation) of mentally disordered offenders is not hindered by forthcoming changes in the arrangements for funding community care: see paragraph 8.12.

4.22. Purchasers should specify suitable quality standards when making non-statutory placements, including the application of "care programme" principles where these would be required if a patient were treated in the NHS. For example, there must be access to a full range of services that may be needed, as well as effective links with local services where "out-of-area" placements are contemplated.

4.23. Similar links must exist between local services and those provided in prisons, Special Hospitals and specialised supra-district or supra-Regional services (CR 3.10-3.13; 3.46; SN 2.8-10).

★ **WE RECOMMEND that the "care programme" principles in Health Circular (90)23/Local Authority Circular (90)11 should be applied explicitly to mentally disordered offenders being cared for and treated by non-statutory services. It should be the duty of purchasers to stipulate this in contracts.**

5

THE MAIN SERVICE FEATURES

Assessment and diversion

5.1. The police have a crucial role as the service which first comes into contact with many mentally disordered suspects (CR 2.4-8). There need to be effective local arrangements between the police, health, social and probation services for the urgent assessment of people who appear to be mentally disordered. These should include (as is now the case in a growing number of areas) a policy on the use of *section 136 of the Mental Health Act* ("removal to a place of safety") and agreement as to health and social services facilities that can be used as places of safety (CR 2.4-13; ST 5.13-15; LD 4.9-11; Mental Health Act *Code of Practice* (1990), Ch 10; Lord Chancellor's Department Best Practice Advisory Group (1992) *Mentally Disordered Offenders*). The possible involvement by the police of an *appropriate adult* under the Police and Criminal Evidence Act 1984 should also be considered (LD 4.11; PACE *Codes of Practice* (2nd ed 1991), Code C, Annex E).

5.2. A person detained under section 136 will not necessarily be suspected of having committed any offence, but, where this may be so or in other cases where a mentally disordered person is suspected of an offence, every effort should be made to ensure that he or she is not drawn unnecessarily into the criminal justice process. For this reason, among others, police stations are not really suitable as places of safety (except perhaps in some outlying rural areas) and suspects should be held there, if at all, for as short a period as possible. Information on the use of section 136 is patchy. Research and better data are needed in this area (CR 4.5-6; ST 5.15; RS 6.8).

5.3. There should be nationwide provision of properly resourced *court assessment and diversion schemes* (see below) and (as is already happening) the further development of *bail information schemes* and *"public interest" case assessment* (PICA) (CR 2.20-25). Some people coming to the attention of these schemes, especially *homeless or rootless people*, who are at particular risk of being remanded in custody on relatively minor charges (CR 3.48; Joseph, *Health Trends* 1990; 2: 51-3; Grounds *et al* (1991) *Mentally Disordered Remanded Prisoners)*, may need access to a range of community provision: see paragraphs 5.11-14 and Annex E. Specialised bail accommodation, with access to health and social services support, should be developed for some mentally disordered people (CR 2.22; *Custody, Care and Justice,* paragraphs 9.7-9) and practical encouragement given to local services to do this.

5.4. Purchasers and providers of health and social services must regard the availability of assessment and diversion schemes as part of a standard service. They must bear in mind also that these services may be needed at any time of day or night and that, given the complex and diverse nature of services and discharge or release patterns (see *figure 1*), *common "entry" or "transfer" mechanisms* (not necessarily at a single point) will help to ensure that people who may need help urgently are not passed from pillar to post (CR 3.31-2; ST 5.40-3).

Court schemes

5.5. By June 1992 there were over 40 court diversion schemes operating in England and over 30 more being planned (Blumenthal/Wessely (1992) *The Extent of Local Arrangements for the Diversion of the Mentally Abnormal Offender from Custody*). However, research suggests that provision for the diversion of mentally disordered offenders is currently planned in fewer than half of district health authorities: see *figures 2 and 3.*

5.6. There is a growing diversity among schemes which we welcome. Some schemes rely on a court psychiatrist (Joseph (1992) *Psychiatric Assessment at the Magistrate's Court;* James/Hamilton *BMJ* 1991; 303; 282-5); some others (for example) use a community psychiatric nurse (CR, Annex D) or a multi-disciplinary "panel" (Circular 66/90, Annex C). In every case, the chosen model must be adapted to local circumstances and effective planning and operational links made with other services and disciplines, including social work. The longer-term future of many schemes is not yet assured, but experience increasingly suggests that, where diversion schemes become established, these come to provide a broader multi-agency focus which, of itself, can make effective disposals easier.

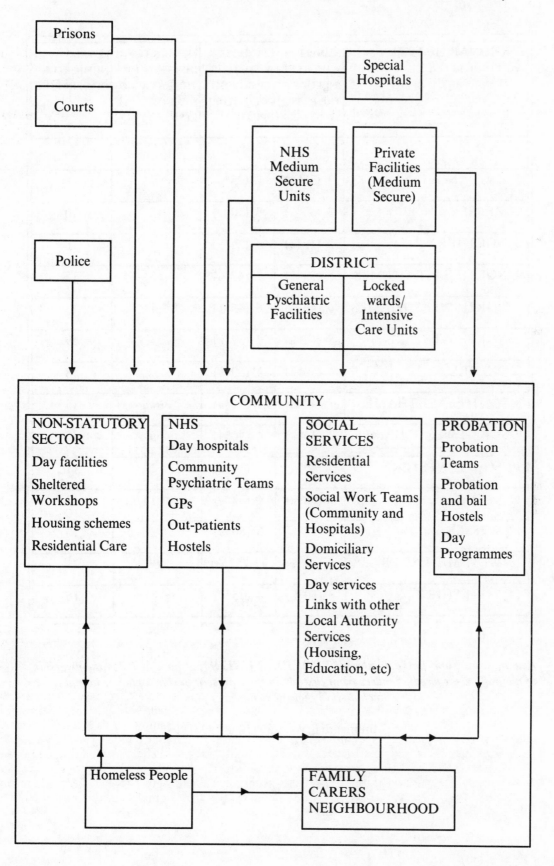

Figure 1

Mentally disordered offenders: Sources of discharge or release into the community

Prisons

Courts

Police

Special Hospitals

NHS Medium Secure Units

Private Facilities (Medium Secure)

DISTRICT

General Pyschiatric Facilities

Locked wards/ Intensive Care Units

COMMUNITY

NON-STATUTORY SECTOR

Day facilities

Sheltered Workshops

Housing schemes

Residential Care

NHS

Day hospitals

Community Psychiatric Teams

GPs

Out-patients

Hostels

SOCIAL SERVICES

Residential Services

Social Work Teams (Community and Hospitals)

Domiciliary Services

Day services

Links with other Local Authority Services (Housing, Education, etc)

PROBATION

Probation Teams

Probation and bail Hostels

Day Programmes

Homeless People

FAMILY CARERS NEIGHBOURHOOD

15

Figure 2

REGIONAL HEALTH AUTHORITIES	NUMBER OF DISTRICTS WHO HAVE OR WILL INCLUDE DIVERSION IN THE PRESENT OR FUTURE PURCHASING PLAN		NUMBER OF DISTRICTS IN THE RHA WHO DID NOT RESPOND	TOTAL NUMBER OF DHAS IN RHA
	Yes	No		
1. EAST ANGLIAN	3 (38%)	2 (25%)	3	8
2. MERSEY	3 (30%)	5 (50%)	2	10
3. NORTHERN	3 (19%)	4 (25%)	9	16
4. NORTH EAST THAMES	5 (33%)	7 (47%)	3	15
5. NORTH WEST THAMES	6 (46%)	6 (46%)	1	13
6. NORTH WESTERN	8 (42%)	7 (37%)	4	19
7. OXFORD	4 (50%)	4 (50%)	0	8
8. SOUTH EAST THAMES	7 (47%)	4 (27%)	4	15
9. SOUTH WEST THAMES	2 (15%)	6 (46%)	5	13
10. SOUTH WESTERN	5 (45%)	4 (36%)	2	11
11. TRENT	7 (58%)	4 (33%)	1	12
12. WESSEX	2 (20%)	6 (60%)	2	10
13. WEST MIDLANDS	4 (19%)	11 (52%)	6	21
14. YORKSHIRE	8 (50%)	4 (25%)	4	16

Regional variations in the number of PROVIDER UNITS that have included the diversion of mentally disordered offenders from custody in their present business plan or intend to include it in their next business plan

Blumenthal/Wessely (June 1992)

Figure 3

REGIONAL HEALTH AUTHORITIES	NUMBER OF DISTRICTS WHO HAVE OR WILL INCLUDE DIVERSION IN THE PRESENT OR FUTURE PURCHASING PLAN		NUMBER OF DISTRICTS IN THE RHA WHO DID NOT RESPOND	TOTAL NUMBER OF DHAS IN RHA
	Yes	No		
1. EAST ANGLIAN	3 (30%)	2 (25%)	4	8
2. MERSEY	3 (38%)	3 (30%)	3	10
3. NORTHERN	3 (19%)	3 (19%)	10	16
4. NORTH EAST THAMES	3 (20%)	6 (40%)	6	15
5. NORTH WEST THAMES	4 (31%)	2 (15%)	7	13
6. NORTH WESTERN	4 (21%)	8 (42%)	7	19
7. OXFORD	1 (13%)	4 (50%)	3	8
8. SOUTH EAST THAMES	7 (47%)	3 (20%)	5	15
9. SOUTH WEST THAMES	4 (31%)	4 (31%)	5	13
10. SOUTH WESTERN	5 (45%)	1 (9%)	5	11
11. TRENT	5 (42%)	5 (42%)	2	12
12. WESSEX	3 (30%)	1 (10%)	6	10
13. WEST MIDLANDS	2 (10%)	7 (33%)	12	21
14. YORKSHIRE	5 (31%)	6 (38%)	5	16

Regional variations in the number of districts that have included the diversion of mentally disordered offenders in their current or next PURCHASING plan

Blumenthal/Wessely (June 1992)

Transport

5.7. Availability of transport to move mentally disordered offenders from one place to another is often a problem (ST 5.44-47; Blumenthal/Wessely, *op cit*). Agencies are sometimes working to different guidelines or making inadequate provision. There is a need to promote greater commonality of approach in this area and to examine the broader aspects of transport provision, including suitability and cost.

★ **WE RECOMMEND that the Department of Health and the Home Office, in conjunction with other agencies, examine the need for consistency in guidance on the operation of transport for mentally disordered offenders and other areas of difficulty, such as the suitability of particular forms of transport and arrangements for funding the movement of patients between agencies.**

Local mental health care and learning disability services

5.8. The National Health Service and Community Care Act 1990 requires health and local authorities to work together in the planning of mental health care services, the main elements of which were described in *Caring for People (op cit)*:

> provision for children and adolescents with psychological problems. This should be primarily community-based, with easy access to a range of professional support and to hospital services (including in-patient treatment if necessary);

> adequate services for the assessment and treatment of adults whose conditions require short term admission to hospital, and for the longer term treatment, including asylum, of those for whom there is no realistic alternative;

> sufficient places in hospital and local authority hostels, sheltered housing, supported lodgings or other similar forms of provision for adults with a mental illness needing residential care outside hospital, together with an adequate range of day and respite services;

> effective co-ordinated arrangements between health and social services authorities, primary health care teams and voluntary agencies for the continuing health and social care of people with a mental illness living in their own homes or in residential facilities. These should include suitable provision for domiciliary services, support to carers, and the training and education of staff working in the community (*ibid*, paragraph 7.3).

Learning disabilities

5.9. The main general service requirements for people with learning disabilities were set out in draft local authority and health circulars issued by the Department of Health in 1991: LD, Annexes D-E. These emphasise that, although social services are seen increasingly as the main agency for planning and arranging services, health authorities have an important continuing role:

> District health authorities should consider contracting for additional services... including specialist assessment and treatment services, in hospital or community settings, where patients with learning disabilities need treatment for psychiatric illness or severe behaviour disturbance that cannot be met adequately within the general psychiatric services; and residential care (or respite care) for people with severe or profound learning disabilities and physical, sensory or psychiatric conditions, where a multi-professional assessment and consultation with parents and carers leads to the conclusion that only the NHS can provide the services they need cost effectively (draft Health Circular, 25 June 1991, paragraph 1).*

The inter-dependency and quality of services

5.10. The tailoring of services to meet individual needs (CR 3.8) means recognising the inter-dependency of services in a range of settings and agencies. Many patients will require a mix of provision. It is the responsibility of both purchasers and providers (see paragraphs 8.2-3) to ensure that the necessary components are in place and are properly co-ordinated (paragraphs 4.10-16). Purchasers must specify quality standards and satisfy themselves that these are being met.

---

*Revised guidance on learning disability services, published since the review ended (Health Service Guidelines (92)42; Local Authority Circular (92)14), retains the broad sense of this secton (LD 1.11-13 and Annexes V-W).

Community services

5.11. It follows from the general principles established in this review that we see community services, possibly augmented in individual cases by other elements (*eg* short-term in-patient or respite care), as providing wherever possible for the majority of mentally disordered offenders.

5.12. The care and treatment needs of mentally disordered offenders in the community will generally be similar to those of non-offenders (CR 3.7-8), but there may be additional aspects requiring assertive follow-up and monitoring. The probation service, for example, is developing its community care role (*Crime, Justice and Protecting the Public* (Cm 965), 1990, paragraphs 7.19-7.22; Home Office Circular 66/90, paragraphs 17-22) and the personal social services as a whole have important preventive and continuing care functions.

5.13. There must be access to a range of *supported and non-supported accommodation* (including independent living, living at home with a family, shared or staffed housing, residential care homes, voluntary hostels, resettlement units and bail hostels: CR 3.21). Merely finding a placement is unlikely to be sufficient. Additional care or support, especially *day care* (CR 3.40), *social security,* and other services, such as *primary or out-patient health care, employment* and *education* (CR 3.39-3.40) will usually be needed.

5.14. We should like to see ***probation orders with a condition of psychiatric treatment*** considered more frequently as an option (CR 3.19). We are pleased that Her Majesty's Inspectorate of Probation intends to examine their relatively low usage (about 1,000 annually) and, more generally, to undertake a "thematic" inspection of the probation service's involvement with mentally disordered offenders. It is possible that ***guardianship orders*** under section 37 of the Mental Health Act will increase with the implementation in October 1992 of section 27 of the ***Criminal Justice Act 1991*** which enables a court to require a local authority to explain whether and how it could exercise such a disposal (CR 3.19; Home Office Circulars 6/1992 and 10/1992). There is also a range of community disposals available under the ***Criminal Procedure (Insanity and Unfitness to Plead) Act 1991*** for the currently very small number of people found unfit to plead (ST 3.51). We welcome these developments.

Hospital services

5.15. There are over 70,000 in-patient beds for people with a mental illness or learning disabilities. Only about 7 per cent. of psychiatric in-patient admissions (about 17,000 of 260,000 in 1989-90) are of people detained under the Mental Health Act. About 85 per cent of these are admitted under Part II of the Act (*ie* not committed by the courts or the Home Secretary) (HR 2.1-2.24): see *figures 4 and 5.*

Local services

5.16. Many offenders needing in-patient care can be accommodated in ordinary psychiatric provision. But, although many offenders can be managed satisfactorily in "open" wards, there must be also better access to local intensive care and locked wards: see ***Annex J.*** According to NHS returns, the number of beds in locked or lockable wards fell from 1,163 for mental illness and 785 for learning disabilities in 1986 to 639 and 274 respectively in 1991. The recent needs assessment exercise suggests that the future requirement for local *low secure provision* may be nearer to the combined 1986 total, but this will need to be confirmed by follow-up with individual Regions.

5.17. All agencies need to be aware that Government policy for re-providing mental illness services (as re-stated in *Caring for People* (*op cit*), the consultative paper, *The Health of the Nation* (Cm 1523, 1991), and very recently in Parliament) does not involve the closure of hospitals as an end in itself (OV 23):

> Our primary aim is not the closure of mental hospitals but the provision of better care for people with mental health problems. Ministers will not approve the closure of any mental hospital unless it can be demonstrated that adequate alternatives have been developed in the community; hence the care programme approach (Baroness Trumpington, House of Lords *Official Report,* 16 June 1992, col. 109).

5.18. We hope that the initiatives arising from the identification of mental illness, including mentally disordered offenders, as a key area in the recent White Paper, *The Health of the Nation* (Cm 1986, 1992) (see paragraph 10.10 below), and the establishment by the Department of Health of a *mental illness task force* under Mr David King (DH Press Releases H92/87 and 92/190) will lead to a more realistic implementation of the re-provision policy.

Medium secure services

5.19. An initial target of 1,000 medium secure hospital beds in *Regional Secure Units* (RSUs) was set in the mid-1970s following the Butler and Glancy reports (see paragraphs 2.6-7 and Health Service Circular (Interim Series)161)). Glancy recommended 1,000 beds; Butler, 2,000 beds. Central capital and revenue funding has been available since then, but the "Glancy" target has not been met. (Full capital funding is available for suitably costed and appraised schemes. In addition to Regions' general revenue allocations, "enhanced" revenue funding for medium secure services currently amounts on average to about £27,000 *per annum* per bed. This is less than half the average cost of an RSU place with associated support services.)

5.20. At 31 January 1992 there were 602 staffed and available beds in permanent RSUs, including 14 for children and adolescents (see *figure 6*). There were some additional 300 beds in facilities regarded by RHAs as *"interim" secure units*, including over 100 for patients with learning disabilities, but not all of these interim places, which were provided pending the development of more permanent facilities, are comparable to those in RSUs, nor could they all be described as providing "medium" security.

5.21. The hospital advisory group recommended that the number of medium secure places should be increased. It considered that at least 1,500 places would be required nationally (HR 5.36).

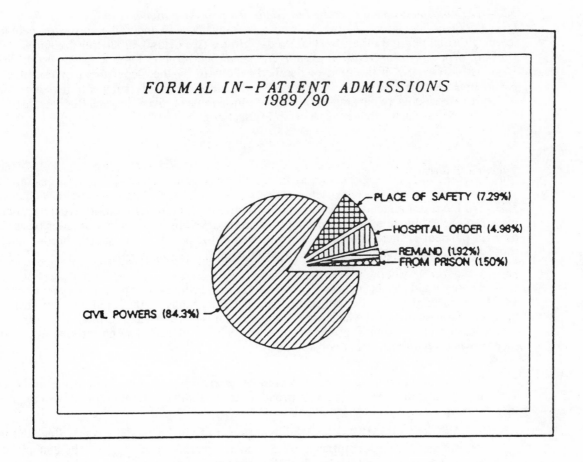

Figure 4: Detained patient admissions compared to
informal psychiatric admissions: 1989/90

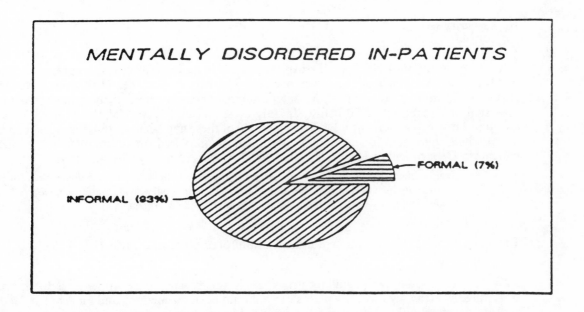

Figure 5: Comparative sources of hospital admission
for detained psychiatric patients

5.22. *The needs assessment exercise has confirmed that the national requirement is likely to be at least 1,500 medium secure places.* However, Regional needs, including those for people with learning disabilities and other "special needs" groups (see below), differ. *We are not proposing a standard proportional increase in existing Regional bed targets.* These must be established for Regions individually in the light of detailed follow-up by the Department of Health of each Regional assessment. As previously proposed, the targets would be subject to review in the light of future assessments. In particular, further attention must be given by some Regions through this process to requirements for learning disability services.

The need to diversify

5.23. We have recommended continuing "earmarked" funding of medium secure services (see paragraph 8.7), but we want to see the programme developed on a much broader basis than to date. In particular, there should be more provision for people with "special needs", including those with learning disabilities or psychopathic disorder (SN 2.16–24).

5.24. There should also be increased provision for those who need care and treatment beyond the 18–24 month limit generally applied to RSU patients. Some of these patients are currently in Special Hospitals due to the lack of suitable medium secure services in the NHS (although the independent sector currently provides some longer-term places). The philosophy and design of such provision requires further consideration.

5.25. We envisage a growing range of *"outreach" provision* so that medium secure units develop as the in-patient component of a much broader service that is better integrated with mainstream care (ST 3.8).

> **WE RECOMMEND that the Department of Health establishes new Regional targets for medium secure provision to reflect assessed need in each Region. These should identify requirements for learning disability and other "special needs" provision and should be kept under review in the light of future needs assessments. Collectively, Regional assessments suggest that at least 1,500 medium secure places will be needed nationally.**

High security services

5.26. There are about 1,700 Special Hospital patients in three locations. Recent research suggests that between 35 per cent and 50 per cent of existing patients may not require high security (Maden *et al,* 1992), although a number of sentenced prisoners may need to be transferred to such provision: see paragraph 5.30 below. In July 1992, about 100 Special Hospital patients were awaiting a move to a more local facility. About 40 of these had been waiting for more than a year despite the requirement for mentally ill and mentally impaired (or severely mentally impaired) patients in Department of Health Circular (88)43/Local Authority Circular (88)14:

> Regional Health Authorities should ensure that no mentally ill special hospital patient [or patient who was or is mentally impaired or severely mentally impaired] who is awaiting a move to a Regional or District facility waits for more than one year (HC(88)43, Appendix 4).

The application of this requirement must be monitored more vigorously (LD 4.19).

5.27. Taking account of the guiding principles of this review, more work needs to be done to establish how many high security places there should be in the medium and longer term, and how and where they should be provided and financed in relation to services for mentally disordered offenders generally.*

---

*Following this review and the *Report of the Committee of Inquiry into Complaints about Ashworth Hospital* (Cm 1986), published on 5 August 1992, a working group on high security and related provision has been established by the Secretary of State for Health. It will report in the Spring of 1993.

Independent hospitals

5.28. There are thought to be about 2,800 beds in the independent sector for the care of mentally ill or learning disabled people. This is a small proportion of the national total. According to health authority returns, there were 88 independent hospitals in 1990-91 registered to detain patients under the Mental Health Act. At 31 March 1990 only 127 detained patients were recorded as being in independent hospitals. (This may well be an under-estimate, given that the comparable 1989 figure was 229, and suggests that some health authorities may not be keeping effective records of their patients.) We drew attention at paragraphs 4.20-22 to the need to develop better links generally with independent services, including the importance of guaranteeing quality and continuity of care, as well as access to a full range of services.

Prison services

5.29. *Prison is unsuitable for a person coming within the scope of the Mental Health Act.*

Figure 6

Medium secure provision:

Permanent Regional Secure Unit places by English Region

Region	Regional Glancy Target	Regional Secure Unit Beds Staffed and Available	
		31/1/92	31/1/91
East Anglian	36	34	34
Mersey	50	36	36
North East Thames	74	14	14
North West Thames	69	46	38
North Western	82	82	82
Northern	62	25	21
Oxford	44	25	39*
South East Thames	72	85	81
South West Thames	58	0†	0
South Western	63	60	60
Trent	91	48	45
Wessex	53	26	26
West Midlands	104	77	77
Yorkshire	71	44	44
TOTAL	929	602	597*

All places are for adult mental illness *except* for 14 child and adolescent beds in North Western Region.

* *This figure includes 14 learning disability beds which were closed on 29 January 1992. Under the terms of Executive Letter (92)6 (see paragraph 2.14), alternative provision was made for the patients concerned.*

†*The Department of Health has approved a 30-bed permanent unit in SW Thames.*

NOTE: **On 31 January 1992 there were 283 staffed and available beds nationally in "interim" secure units (see paragraph 5.20). Some of these provide medium security and some for patients with learning disabilities.**

5.30. Research by Gunn *et al* (*op cit*) suggests that between 750 and 1,400 sentenced prisoners may currently require transfer to hospital for psychiatric treatment. There are others on remand who might have been diverted before or when they came to court (PR 3.2-6; Grounds *et al, op cit*). However effectively diversion schemes operate, there will still be prisoners who develop signs of mental illness while in prison, and many who have continuing mental health care needs but are not sufficiently ill to warrant transfer to hospital. Gunn *et al* found that 38 per cent of their sample of adult male prisoners and 59 per cent of female prisoners (the latter mainly due to a higher incidence of neuroses and drug abuse) had a psychiatric diagnosis, but that the majority did not meet the criteria for hospital admission under the Mental Health Act. The prevalence of prisoners with learning disabilities may be as low as 1-2 per cent (LD 4.22), but needs often go unidentified or unmet.

Contracting for mental health care services

5.31. The decision, which we strongly support, to contract in to prisons a full mental health care service from the NHS (DPMS (1991) *Contracting for Prison Health Services,* paragraphs 3.16-3.21; OV, Annex C; PR 5.30), initially for remand prisoners, will have considerable practical and resource implications, which are considered in the reports of the prison and staffing and training advisory groups. This is part of a much wider programme by which the Health Care Service for Prisoners (formerly the Prison Medical Service) will become a purchaser rather than a provider of health care generally. We welcome the pilot projects that are planned, some with a mental health element.

5.32. For prisoners with mental health care needs, including those on remand, this change of approach should lead to:
- i. better quality care;
- ii. prompter assessments, which we recommend should be subject to agreed targets (a minimum of 90 per cent of cases within 14 days; 50 per cent within 7 days: PR 3.12-13); and
- iii. through effective discharge and care programme arrangements (PR 5.33-38; St 5.30-35), continuity of care on release or transfer to hospital.

5.33. However, a proper therapeutic approach will be possible only if there are also improvements in prison conditions and regimes generally (as envisaged in *Custody, Care and Justice, op cit:* OV, Annex D) and attention to such practical requirements as the needs of visiting professional staff (CR 3.13). The prison advisory group made detailed recommendations for improving the standard of mental health care.

6

THE STAFFING AND TRAINING IMPLICATIONS

6.1. The staffing and training advisory group analysed in detail the current and prospective inputs of the various professional disciplines to work with mentally disordered offenders. It also considered the specialised and more general training needs of staff at basic and post-qualifying levels. The special needs group did likewise for staff working with offenders with learning disabilites (LD 7.7-34).

Anticipating growth within developing specialties

6.2. It is difficult at present to identify precise contributions to work with offenders, although there is reasonably reliable information on the staffing of secure services. For the future, staffing estimates must be based on the outcome of local needs assessments (ST 1.10), although there will be a continuing role nationally for the Department of Health and the Home Office and some other bodies (*eg* the Royal College of Psychiatrists) which are responsible for recommending staffing levels for specific functions.

6.3. Similarly, we envisage a mainly "employer-led" approach to the determination of training needs, with an important role therefore for all agencies, including Regional Health Authorities within the framework of the NHS Management Executive's *Working Paper 10* (ST 4.4 and Annex L). The development of a sound academic base will be an essential part of this process (see paragraphs 7.2-7). But, here again, a good deal of coordination will also be required nationally, especially among and within the main training bodies and teaching institutions, if sufficient staff are to be trained to work in growing specialties.

6.4. *Forensic psychiatry,* for example, has developed from virtually a nil base within a generation, but we anticipate more than a doubling of consultant numbers (at least 80 in addition to the present 70), plus increases in *other consultant psychiatrists* of over twice that number and training posts to support them (ST 3.34-6). *Clinical psychology* numbers in the forensic field may need more than to double in the next five years (ST 3.44), while *therapy* (occupational, physio-, and speech and language therapy) and *education* services require further development, in particular within secure services (ST 3.47; 3.69-72). *Forensic nursing* is an under-developed specialty in which recognised academic training (now available in three centres) has been slow to develop. Yet the likely growth in nursing numbers as a whole is probably more than that of the other disciplines combined (ST 3.37-42; 4.24-5). A major review of mental health nursing will begin in September 1992 (Department of Health Press Release H92/225).

6.5. In the community field, *social services and probation staff* will require relevant expertise to contribute to a range of multi-agency activities (ST 4.49-61). We propose an increase in the Training Support Programme for social services (see paragraph 8.11). In the courts and elsewhere in the *criminal justice system*, a range of staff, from judges downwards, need to be encouraged and trained to develop a better understanding of the needs of mentally disorded offenders (ST 4.62-9). More *interpreters* with specialised training are required to assist mentally disorded offenders with certain special needs (*eg* people from ethnic minorities and those with a hearing impairment) (SN 2.37)

6.6. The development of the *Health Care Service for Prisoners* also presents major training implications, including the encouragement of greater specialisation and opportunities for work in prison as part of professional training. We welcome the recent report of the Royal Colleges of Physicians, General Practitioners and Psychiatrists on the education and training of doctors in prison health care work (ST 4.16).

Additional staffing needs

6.7. We have estimated at *figure 7* minimum *additional* staffing needs by discipline. These take account of contributions to mental health care in prisons, as well as developments in hospital and community services and educational needs (ST 3.74).

6.8. There will be further requirements for people working with patients with particular "special needs", although some of these (for example, staff working in secure units with learning disabled patients) are accouted for in the broad projections.

6.9. The implications for the development of *medium secure units*, in particular, are considerable. Upwards of 2,800 staff in all disciplines may need to be appointed if at least 1,500 beds are to be opened with a full range of "outreach" services (although some of these staff will be available through re-provision) (ST 3.8-11).

The interface between professions

6.10. The growth of multi-agency arrangements should lead to a growing commonality of interests between the various professions. That does not mean that professional boundaries will (or should) disappear, but rather that there will be greater flexibility and versatility, and a better understanding of complementary interests and skills. In particular, there will be a number of common training needs, for example, in respect of "special needs" groups (SN 2.40), *racial and cultural issues* (ST 5.5-7; SN 3.13), *risk assessment* (ST 5.36-7) and *responses to violence* (ST 5.38), and *potential suicides* (SN 4.13). There will also be the opportunity to reassess staff mixes to take account of a range of factors (*eg* the development of more broadly-based services and the needs of *woman patients*). We have not assumed that the mix will be as before, although present staffing patterns, adjusted where necessary to take account of anticipated diversity, tend to provide the main basis for broad interim projections of the future staffing requirement.

6.11. Inter-professional areas requiring particular attention are the interface between *forensic and general psychiatry* and between *social work and probation.* There is already widespread, though patchy, contact between general psychiatry and the criminal justice system (Blumenthal/Wessely, *op cit;* Bartlett *et al* (1992) *The NHS and the Penal and Criminal Justice Systems: Evaluation of the Interfaces—Interim Report*); ST 2.12): see *figure 8.* This needs to be developed and extended. There are moves towards closer working between social work and probation. Discussions at chief officer level and between the Social Services and Probation Inspectorates, begun through the review, will continue (ST 4.58-61).

Figure 7

Estimated minimum needs for additional staff

MEDICAL	At least 80 additional consultant forensic psychiatrist posts, plus 175 other consultant posts and 10–15 consultant posts for academic work. All supported by additional senior registrar, registrar and junior posts. Enhanced input by general practitioners and development of the role of psychotherapists.
NURSING	Over 2,000 nursing posts to be filled in medium secure services, with additional needs in local hospitals, prisons and the community.
PSYCHOLOGY	At least 80 additional clinincal psychologists over the next 5 years.
THERAPISTS AND INTERPRETERS	Enhanced provision of occupational therapy, speech therapy and physiotherapy, with early priority to expansion in Special Hospitals and medium secure units. Also a requirement for interpreters (SN 2.37).
SOCIAL SERVICES	At least 125 whole time equivalent social workers for work in medium secure units and court diversion schemes, with additional needs for a variety of social services staff in a range of settings, including those working in residential, day and domiciliary care and in prisons.
PROBATION SERVICES	At least 130 whole time equivalent probation officers to deal with mental disorder cases in bail information and PICA schemes and to work in multi-agency teams and (on secondment) in medium secure units.
EDUCATION	At about 110 posts *in toto* to work in medium secure units. There will be further requirements in other settings and to contribute to multi-agency teams.

See Chapter 3 of the report of the staffing and training advisory group

Figure 8

**Contacts by a sample of general psychiatrists or
their staff with the criminal justice system**

(January/February 1992)

*QUESTION: How often do you, or a designated member of your psychiatric team, visit a
local police station, a magistrates' court and/or remand prison to perform psychiatric
assessments with the purpose of diverting mentally disordered offenders from custody?*

FREQUENCY	Police Station [per cent of sample who visit]	Magistrates' court	Remand prison
Weekly	5%	1%	1%
Fortnightly	8%	1%	3%
Monthly	14%	2%	2%
Less than monthly	57%	30%	57%
Not in the last 12 months or never	15%	66%	38%
Sample = 136			

Blumenthal/Wessely (1992)

**Note: These figures are based on a slightly larger sample (136) than that (128) used in figure
3 of the report of the staffing and training advisory group. Annex E of that report contains
more detailed data on the contribution by the sample to work with mentally disordered
offenders.**

THE ACADEMIC AND RESEARCH BASE

7.1. The effective development and operation of services for mentally disordered offenders requires a sound academic and research base. This base is at present poorly developed and requires corrective action from the centre.

Academic Development

The present base

7.2. The present academic base for forensic psychiatry and related disciplines is too small. It has not kept pace with the expansion of services nor training needs (AD 2.2).

7.3. In England the only academic posts supported through Higher Education Funding Council money in a department of forensic psychiatry are a professor and a lecturer at the Institute of Psychiatry in London and part of a university lecturer (consultant) post at Cambridge. There is a personal Chair in forensic psychiatry at the University of Birmingham, academic sections led by senior lecturers at St Bartholomew's and St George's Hospitals in London, and several lecturer posts elsewhere, including the Special Hospitals (AD 2.3-6), mostly funded by the NHS.

7.4. There are Chairs in psychiatric social work at Manchester University and clinical psychology at Birmingham University (where the present incumbent has a special interest in forensic psychology). There are other academic posts in psychology which maintain an interest in forensic matters. There is an academic nursing post at Liverpool University with links to Ashworth Special Hospital, but, as noted at paragraph 6.4, forensic psychiatric nursing as a discipline is under-developed (AD 2.11-16).

The future

7.5. There should be a clear policy of encouraging the development of multi-disciplinary academic departments. These will need a full infrastructure. There needs to be a better geographical spread, although not at the expense of existing expertise (AD 3.1-7). Professional bodies, Regional advisers in forensic psychiatry, the Special Hospitals Service Authority and the private sector all need to be involved in the process of developing new links.

7.6. We understand that the Department of Health and the Home Office have had preliminary discussions with the Department for Education about charting a way forward. Given the DFE's existing "arm's length" relationship with the Universities (AD 5.6), a key part of the process of development will be to stimulate directly the interest of academic institutions, including departments in related disciplines such as criminology or law, in expanding their work in the area of mentally disordered offenders.

The health care of prisoners

7.7. The prison population differs significantly from the population as a whole in the incidence (often higher) of psychiatric and physical morbidity. The plans for changes in the delivery of health care for prisoners and the need for better knowledge of the clinical issues involved all point to a strengthening of the academic and research contribution. We have recommended the establishment of an academic department in the health care of prisoners.

Research

The framework

7.8. The establishment of a more extensive academic base must be accompanied by a more positive and coordinated approach to research on mentally disordered offenders in a range of settings. "Research is essential to any strategy to improve health" (*The Health of the Nation* (1992), *op cit,* paragraph 5.4).

7.9. We propose the establishment of a national committee to set research priorities and oversee the development of a strategy (RS 2.10; 3.10). This would be underpinned by a network of reasonably well-spread core departments, integrating both clinical and research services (RS 4.4). There should be greater attention to the dissemination of results (RS 5.4).

Subject areas

7.10. A range of research topics which might form part of a strategic plan are set out in matrix form at *figure 9.* In addition, we suggest as priorities for learning disability research the role of secure provision, prevalence of learning disabilities among the remand prison population and a process study of offending (LD 8.2). The need for secure child and adolescent provision should also be researched (SN, Paper 6).

NHS R & D strategy

7.11. The plan will need to take account of other recent developments, including the research and development strategy for the NHS, launched in April 1992, and the setting of priorities for NHS mental health research (Department of Health Press Release H92/193), which do not include offenders as such but are all of potential relevance:

    i.   severely mentally ill people: community care and quality of residential care;

    ii.   training packages for use with those working in primary care in the community;

    iii.   the mental health of the NHS workforce;

    iv.   methods of establishing the mental health needs of the population.

Figure 9: **Possible components of a strategic plan for research on mentally disordered offenders**

TOPIC	SOCIAL POLICY	BASIC RESEARCH IN MEDICINE ETC	SERVICE DELIVERY	LEGAL AND PENAL PRACTICE
Mentally Disordered Offenders	Relationships between-prevalence of offending by mentally disordered and social deprivation	Epidemiological surveys by NHS Region. Longitudinal studies of MDOs. Dev. of drug treatments	Provision of services by general psychiatrists. Quality of aftercare in community	Use of hospital/guardianship/probation orders or prison sentences
Personality Disorders	Environmental factors which influence personality disorder	*Literature review *Treatability issues *Diagnostic issues	*Evaluation of treatment	Use of hospital/prison disposals
Sexual Offenders		*Distinction between sexual disorders and sexual offending. Epidemiolical survey in UK	*Roles of penal health and social services	Effect of changes in law
Violent Offenders	Effect on victims	Relation to mental disorder Treatment programmes in prison and community	Evaluation of treatment programmes	
Police		Profiling offenders	*Services required to assist police to identify MDO's	*Use of section 136
Community Services		Effect of the reprovision of local services on mental health	*Effect of social supervision of restricted patients	
Prisoners		*Prevalence of mental disorder in remand prison population	Arrangements for mental health services for prisoners	Measures to prevent suicide or self harm
Adolescents	Effect of disturbed childhood on later incidence of mental disorder/offending	Indicators of future offending (especially sexual offending)	Evaluation of current interventions (especially sexual offending)	Pathways into custody of juveniles (effects of new child and CJ legislation)
Diversion	Attitudes of prison officers to MDOs. Public attitude to not prosecuting mentally disordered		*Resources required for effective diversion schemes	MHA sections—suitability of, for diverting MDOs from CJ system. Power of judges/magistrates
Hospital Services	*Outcome indicators for hospital care		*Assessment of needs for different types of hospital provision	
Women		Prevalence of mental disorder	Availability/use of services	Differential use of hospital orders
Ethnic Minorities		*Evaluation of treatment approaches and responses	*Availability/use of services *Equitable treatment of Ethnic Minorities	

*Recommended priority (RS 6.8)

8

THE FINANCIAL IMPLICATIONS

8.1. The resource implications of this review are considerable. Much could be achieved through better coordination and more effective use of resources, but we are recommending substantial service development which, taken as a whole, cannot be met within existing resources. We have also looked at the ways in which services are financed currently by a range of agencies to see whether resources could be used better or targeted more effectively. In particular, we have considered the effects of the new "purchaser/provider" arrangements in the NHS and similar arangements to be introduced for local authority social services in 1993.

Purchasers and providers

8.2. *Purchasing* includes not simply obtaining a service, but also assessing need, service development, financial planning, setting budgets and priorities, specifying and monitoring service and performance standards, placing contracts and meeting "extra-contractual" referrals (FN 5.2). It is, in many respects, the crucial function if services for mentally disordered offenders are to be improved. What we found during the review suggests that more needs to be done to engage and inform the interest of many (though by no means all) purchasers.

8.3. *Providers* are bodies in the statutory or non-statutory sectors who provide services under contract. Many are becoming increasingly entrepreneurial, although the extent to which mentally disordered offenders will benefit as a result depends on whether their particular specialised needs are among those that providers want to meet.

8.4. There is thus a lot of uncertainty at present. It was for that reason that we recommended the interim protection of services for mentally disordered offenders (see paragraph 2.14).

"What about resources?"

8.5. The staffing and training advisory group summarised some of the major resource issues as follows:

> No doubt some changes could be achieved (indeed, already are being achieved in many areas) through more effective use of resources, in particular through closer multi-agency working. New arrangements for purchasing services may assist in some instances, though many potential patients are currently a charge to the criminal justice system and would therefore be an additional call on the health and social services. This review itself, and the Home Office Circular 66/90 immediately before it, have helped to raise the public, political and service profile of mentally disordered offenders ... This may serve to stimulate a "bottom up" increase in expenditure relative to other local priorities.
>
> But establishing a better framework, essential though it is, and even if coupled with some new resources found from within current allocations, cannot offer a complete solution ... The development of shared systems, new methods of purchasing, and more productive liaison are really only a starting point.
>
> Specialised services for many mentally disordered offenders are highly labour-intensive. The care and treatment of perhaps the majority of offenders within mainstream services will have implications for those services; it cannot be assumed ... that they could simply absorb an influx of new patients. The increase in capital funding for new medium secure places from £3 million in 1991-92 to £18 million in 1992-3 is very welcome, but it needs to be borne in mind that achievement of even the existing target of 1,000 beds may require the appointment of well over 1,000 staff. The contracting-in of mental health care services to prisons cannot be done within existing financial or staffing resources if patients are to receive the equality of care envisaged in last year's prison White Paper *(Custody, Care and Justice, op cit)*. Nor can it be taken for granted that "care programmes" will ensure that patients diverted or discharged from the criminal justice system will receive the co-ordinated care they need; the operation and resourcing of such arrangements for mentally disordered offenders need careful attention.
>
> Time and again in the course of this review the question has been asked, *"what about resources?"* ... (ST 1.14-17).

"Well, this certainly scuppers our plan to conquer the Universe".

8.6. We have not put an overall price tag on the developments recommended in this review. Much will depend on local needs assessments. The pace at which change can proceed is not simply a question of how much money is available. There will inevitably be lead-in times for training, capital planning and so forth. The sheer scale of the changes recommended dictates that Rome will not be built in a day. However, things must certainly move more quickly than they did after the Butler and Glancy reports and the momentum that has developed through the review must be sustained.

Key Issues

Health services

8.7. The finance advisory group considered both the cost implications of the recommendations made by the earlier service advisory groups and the need for a more integrated approach to finance across a number of agencies. It identified as key issues to be tackled for health services:

    i. *the breaking down of disincentives* to suitable placements, in particular the fact that disposals which are most likely to meet a patient's needs often involve transfers between agencies that, in financial terms, may be unwelcome to the receiving agency (FN 2.11). Reducing the number of purchasers (eg district health authorities paying for all hospital-based care, including that in Special Hospitals) would be one way of promoting this objective (FN 5.6-7; Bynoe (MIND, 1992) *Treatment, Care and Security);*

    ii. *the responsibility of district health authorities,* subject to effective performance management (see paragraphs 8.17-19) and monitoring arrangements both Regionally and nationally, for purchasing a full range of specialised services assessed as being needed by their populations (FN 5.7). This does not imply that only single districts would be purchasers. They may exercise this function, for example, as part of health consortia or jointly with other agencies. The key word is "responsibility";

    iii. *mechanisms to maintain specialised services* that will continue to be needed, possibly, in some instances, on a supra-district or supra-Regional basis (FN 3.6; SN 2.9-15). The NHS Management Executive and the NHS are currently looking at possible solutions to recognised difficulties in this area, including the development of "insurance premium" contracts and funding through Regional contracts;

    iv. *earmarking funds for "exceptional" needs such as the medium secure unit programme* (see paragraphs 5.19-25). Arrangements already exist for the central funding of up to 1,000 medium secure places. We are aware of the attention being given to developing the methodology for allocating capital funds to the NHS as a whole. However, given the level of capital and revenue investment needed to increase the number of beds rapidly to at least 1,500, we regard continued earmarking as the best means of achieving this goal. We see the need also for a less complicated approach to "enhanced" revenue funding and propose that a flat rate per bed is substituted for an existing formula whereby Regions receive extra money at differential rates once they reach two-thirds of their medium secure bed target.

8.8. Underlying these issues are two important principles:

    i.   that planning decisions about services for mentally disordered offenders should take account of the cost *to all agencies,* including the future cost of deterioration in a person's condition if needs are not met properly (FN 2.5; LD 7.4);

    ii. that decisions about the admission or transfer of patients should be based *solely on clinical needs and public safety.*

8.9. If not already known, the agency responsible for payment should be established as soon as possible after admission. Where there is doubt as to the "home district", the regulations at *Annex K* apply.

Community services

Local authorities

8.10. For local authorities, we propose an increase in the *mental illness specific grant* (whose value is £31.4 million in 1992-93) to recognise the particular needs of mentally disordered offenders (FN 6.12-15). We believe that the grant-aided element of this should be fully-funded (as opposed to 70 per cent at present) (FN 6.17). Extending the specific grant would help to support:

    i.   social work involvement in assessment, diversion, "out-of-area" case conferences, secure psychiatric care and multi-agency teams;

    ii. residential and day services;

    iii. care programmes for discharged prisoners and those remitted to prison from hospital (see paragraph 4.16).

8.11. We recommend also increases in *supplementary credit approvals* for capital development (FN 6.20) and in the social services *Training Support Programme* (SN 5.57 and paragraph 6.4 above).

8.12. We are particularly concerned that the transfer to local authorities from 1993-94 of social security funds currently used to meet the cost of accommodation should not work to the disadvantage of mentally disordered offenders. We welcome the intention of the Department of Health to issue guidance on "ordinary residence" which may be helpful in some potentially difficult cases. However, looking at the broader issue, the concerns expressed to us by voluntary organisations and others are such that we believe the Government may need to consider taking positive action, possibly through the introduction of a specific grant, to ensure that access to services is safeguarded.

8.13. More generally we consider that the issues emerging from this review should be discussed with the Department of the Environment and the Housing Corporation (FN 6.31).

    ★ **WE RECOMMEND that the Department of Health and other Government Departments with a direct interest in the accommodation for mentally disordered offenders in the community take early co-ordinated action to ensure that access to such accommodation is not jeopardised by forthcoming changes in the financing of community care.**

Other agencies

8.14. There will be financial implications for other agencies, especially for the staffing of the *probation services* (FN 6.24), if community services are to be developed on a multi-agency basis, although the overall effect on the police should be financially neutral (SN 3.62). We want to see the greater involvement of *voluntary agencies* encouraged through the availability of an annual sum for services for mentally disordered offenders remanded from courts, discharged from hospital or released from prison (FN 6.28). The cost of enhancing the *primary care* role is difficult to estimate, but there certainly will be resource needs in some areas where social conditions are poor and incidence of mental disorder high (FN 6.34). General practitioners already see an estimated nine million people with mental health problems every year (ST 2.16).

8.15. The flexible use of community resources should be encouraged, including pooled (or at any rate better co-ordinated) resources and joint purchasing (FN 6.39-41).

Academic development

8.16. As described at paragraphs 7.2-7, there needs to be a more coherent and positive approach to the financing of academic development. This is essential to the underpinning of service development, training and research.

Performance management

8.17. Performance management is important in terms both of making effective use of resources and ensuring that agreed objectives are met. To this end:
    i.   local multi-agency groups need to develop the capacity to monitor performance across the range of services (FN 4.8);
    ii.   performance indicators on services for mentally disordered offenders should be developed and piloted (FN 4.8; CR 4.11-13). *Figure 10* suggests a possible set of input, process and outcome indicators on prevention and diversion (FN, Annex F; ST 5.22): see also Jenkins, *Brit J Psychiat* (1990) 157, 500-514; Standing Medical Advisory Committee (1991) *The Quality of Medical Care; The Health of the Nation* (1992, *op cit*), Annex C.
    iii.   there should be further work to develop methods for carrying out spot service audits (FN 4.8);
    iv.   "multi-axial" (*ie* physical, psychological, social, *etc*) assessments currently being developed for general psychiatric services might usefully be adapted to offender services (FN, Annex F).

8.18. The performance management group of this review is to be kept in being to help spearhead this work.

8.19. *The Health of the Nation* has set specific targets for:
    a.   improving significantly the health and social functioning of mentally ill people; and
    b.   the reduction of the overall *suicide rate* by at least 15 per cent by 2000 and that of severely mentally ill people by at least a third.

Statistics

8.20. Further work is needed nationally to examine the central collection of statistics, including the need for consistency between data collected by the Department of Health and the Home Office and the scope for covering such aspects as ethnicity (FN 4.8; SN 3.13).

The cartoon below paragraph 8.5 is reproduced from *Private Eye* by kind permission. The drawing above paragraph 8.19 is from *Executive Agencies – A Guide to Setting Targets and Measuring Performance* (1992) by permission of HM Treasury.

Figure 10: **Prevention and diversion indicators for mentally disordered offenders**

Local Objective	Service Objective	Service Unit	Service Input	Service Output	Service Outcome	Health and Social Outcome
To reduce the possibility of ever becoming an MDO, by early identification and treatment of mental disorder with assertive monitoring.	Identify early signs of mental disorder as soon as possible. Monitor via <u>care programme.</u>	GPs, social worker, CPNs, Mental Health Unit, other key worker, forensic psychiatrist, psychiatrist, access to DLW, RSU, SH. Voluntary agencies.	Identify those at risk. Educate the patient and his carers. Treat Monitor (cure programme) Manpower, education, research, training.	– Numbers identified – Numbers treated – Numbers monitored.	% correctly identified (% missed) % appropriately monitored % who fall out of care (care programme).	– Reduce incidence and prevalence of offending amongst mentally disordered.
To increase the proportion of mentally disordered offenders diverted to health and social services care <u>before</u> entry into CJS pre-arrest or arrest.	Identify MDO and divert to hospital or community.	police psychiatrist (Gen, For/C&A/LD) mental health unit DLW, RSU, SH social worker duty solicitor community placements (hostel etc.) housing dept. voluntary agencies.	Identify those at risk. Close links between police and psychiatrists and other agencies. Manpower, training. Local S136 policy and 24 hour duty rotas for psychs, S12 doctors system. Care programme.	– Numbers identified – Numbers diverted: Informally under S2, S3, S4 S136.	% correctly identified (%.missed) % diverted effectively (measure with suitable scale?)	– Reduce numbers of suicides in prison – Reduced risk of prolonging episode of illness by maximising opportunity for early intervention. – reduced risk to the public of harm.
To increase the proportion of mentally disordered offenders diverted to health and social services care <u>before</u> entry into the CJS from the police cells.	Identify MDO and divert to hospital or community.	police, duty solicitor, probation, psychiatrist (as above) social worker, voluntary agencies, CPS mental health unit, DLW, RSU, SH community placements (hostel etc) housing dept. Transport to hospital.	Identify MDOs at risk. Care programme. Manpower, training, education. Multi-agency working. Local S136 policy, 24 hr duty rota for psychs. S12 system for doctors.	– Numbers identified – Numbers diverted: informally under S2, S3, S4 S136.	% correctly identified % correctly diverted (effectiveness of diversion—measure with suitable scale. One factor would be time).	– Reduce homelessness – Reduce numbers of suicides in prison – Reduce risk to the public of harm – Reduce prevalence of mental disorder in the prison popn. – Decrease numbers of MDOs in police cells.

Local Objective	Service Objective	Service Unit	Service Input	Service Output	Service Outcome	Health and Social Outcome
To increase the proportion of MDOs diverted to health and social servies after entry into CJS from the courts.	Identify MDO and divert to hospital or the community.	Probation, magistrates, judges, duty solicitor, CPS, psychiatrist (as above) social worker, mental health unit, DLW, RSU, SH. Community placement (hostel etc), housing dept. Transport to hospital/community Room at court to interview.	Identify those at risk. Care programme, Manpower, training, education policies. Court diversion scheme. Multiagency working, S12 system for doctors, SW duty system.	– Numbers identified. – Numbers diverted: Informally discontinuence probation with condition treatment S2, S3, S35, S36, S37.	% correctly identified % correctly diverted (effectiveness of diversion—measure with suitable scale. One factor would be time.)	– Reduce suicides in prison – Reduce prevalence of mental disorder in prison population (spot audit) – Reduce homelessness – Reduce numbers of MDOs with "case dismissed" and no follow up.
To increase the proportion of MDOs diverted from health and social services after entry into CJS from prisons.	Identify MDO and divert to hospital or the community.	Health care service for prisoners (including doctors and health care workers) mental health unit, DLW, RSU, SH, CPS, C3, HO, Courts Mag. and Judges, Psychiatrist (gen/for/C&A/LD) CPN, SW, psychologist.	Identify MDO at risk. Suitable reception screening and throughcare (Health Care Standard). Care programme, Training, Manpower, Education Policies. Multiagency working. Screening for sentenced popn.	– Numbers of psych. court reports. – Numbers identified – Numbers diverted: S35, S36, S48, S47 (Governor's order).	% correctly identified % correctly diverted % identified and diverted within specific time.	– Reduce numbers of suicides in prison – Reduce prevalence of mental disorder in prison population (spot audit).
To reduce the relapse and possibility of reoffending with re-entry into the CHS by ensuring appropriate follow-up and care after diversion, discharge or release.	To enable the MDO to be "plugged" into care programme.	Health care service for prisoners, police, probation magistrates, judge, psychiatrist (for/gen/C&A/LD) SW, Mental health unit, DLW, RSU, SH, CPN, housing dept. hostels, day care outpatients.	Identify MDO multiagency working to ensure assessment and placement prior to discharge/release or transfer. Care programme, key worker, Training, Education, Manpower policies.	– Numbers "plugged" in to care programme on discharge/release/ diversion.	% correctly identified % who fall out of care.	– Reduce reoffending – Reduce risk to public of harm. – Increase health and social functioning (multi-axial measure to be developed) – Reduce prevalence of mental disorder in prison population – Reduce homelessness amongst MDOs.

9

THE LAW

9.1. This is not a review of the law. However, we were invited to make any recommendations which we felt would help to further the objectives of the review.

The need to promote suitable and speedy disposals

9.2. The preceding chapters have been concerned largely with measures to improve the level, range and operation of services for mentally disordered offenders. Against this backgound, we see it as important that the relevant legislation helps to promote—or, at the very least, does not hinder—the objective of ensuring suitable and speedy disposals for people in need (possibly urgent need) of psychiatric assessment or treatment. As such, there are some difficulties which we think need to be addressed.

9.3. An example is where, despite clinical advice, a court is unable to make a hospital order under the Mental Health Act 1983 because NHS purchasers or providers cannot, for whatever reason, find a bed. In other instances, a power may be reserved to a Crown Court, whereas a magistrates' court, possibly with access to one of the increasing number of assessment and diversion schemes (see paragraphs 5.5–6), is limited in the disposals it can make.

9.4. The possible consequence in both cases is that the accused person may be remanded to prison for psychiatric reports or be sentenced to imprisonment despite his or her medical condition. The findings by Gunn *et al* (see paragraph 5.30) indicate the level of unsuitable prison disposals. A further indication (though obviously welcome in a sense) is the increasing number of prisoners (470 in 1991) transferred to hospital for treatment under section 47 or 48 of the Mental Health Act. Another is that, at any one time, about 100 mentally disordered prisoners are awaiting transfer to an NHS hospital (101 in June 1992). There are also, as we have noted, a number of mentally disordered people accommodated unsuitably in the hospital system, in particular in Special Hospitals (see paragraph 5.26).

Suggested legal changes in step with service development

9.5. We recognise that any legal changes must be linked to the broader service development proposals emerging from this review. Simply changing the law will not of itself offer quickfire solutions. New provisions could, in some instances, actually be harmful to patient care or public safety if they were not properly resourced or if the health or social services were not in a position to provide for the consequences. However, legal measures which go hand-in-hand with service development can offer an important lever for ensuring that the caring agencies meet their responsibilities towards mentally disordered offenders.

9.6. The following possibilities, for futher consideration by the Department of Health, the Home Office and other interested bodies, have emerged from the work of the advisory groups and our own discussions:

to assist suitable disposals by the court

i. in the light of our observations at paragraph 9.3, to enable the courts, in exceptional cases, to direct the admission of an accused person to hospital (*eg* to avoid a patently unsuitale custodial disposal where a health authority seems disinclined to purchase a suitable bed and the pressing medical need is unquestionable);

ii.   a. to enable a hospital to give treatment, if necessary, under *section 35 of the Mental Health Act*. At present this permits Crown Courts and, in specified circumstances, magistrates' courts to remand an accused or convicted person to hospital for assessment only;

    b. to enable magistrates, in common with the Crown Courts, to remand for hospital treatment, under *section 36* (PR 3.3);

iii. to remove or restrict powers to remand to prison for the primary purpose of medical assessment under the *Bail Act 1976* and the *Magistrates' Courts Act 1980* (PR 3.3).

to assist hospital transfers

iv.   a. to extend the ambit of *sections 36 and 48 of the Mental Health Act* (which permit the transfer to hospital of an accused person suffering from mental illness or severe mental impairment) to include people with mental impairment or psychopathic disorder (PR 3.7–11). This would reflect our view that a person requiring treatment for any kind of mental disorder within the scope of the Act should receive it as soon as practicable;

      b. with this in mind, we are concerned also that the requirement under *section 48* that the need for treatment should be "urgent" is often interpreted narrowly (Grounds *et al, op cit*). We think that it should be applied where a doctor would recommend in-patient treatment if a person were seen as an out-patient in the community;

v. to enable prisoners to be transferred to hospital under *sections 47 or 48* for assessment as well as treatment. It is not always feasible for thorough assessments to be undertaken in prison; a hospital can usually offer greater flexibility and specialised expertise, especially in cases where diagnosis is problematic;

vi. to give the Secretary of State power to direct the transfer of a restricted patient between hospitals. We see this as helping to encourage, in suitable cases, transfers to less secure provision, as well as minimising the use of trial leave from one hospital as a device for testing the water in a second.

9.7. In making these proposals, we are aware that the Mental Health Act in particular struck a careful balance between a number of factors, including those relating to personal liberty, and that any one amendment could have implications for other sections. Any wider effects would require careful thought.

★ **WE RECOMMEND that the Department of Health, the Home Office and other interested bodies consider the suggestions at paragraph 9.6 for changes to the law, including any consequential effects that these might have on other parts of the present legislation. Any changes should move in tandem with service developments.**

Compulsory supervision in the community

9.8. We have not considered in detail the notion of enabling compulsory supervision to be given to a mentally disordered patient in the community. This is a contentious issue whose implications are wider than the scope of this review. A number of bodies and reports have given opinions on the issue in recent years. The Royal College of Psychiatrists is currently examining the implications. Before too long, the Government will need to take a view.

Mental incapacity and consent

9.9. The Law Commission has completed a thorough examination of the law on mental incapacity and consent to treatment (*Mentally Incapacitated Adults and Decision-Making* (1991): *Discussion Paper 119;* CR 3.19; LD 5.24). Taken as a whole, this also extends beyond the scope of the review, but forms part of the increasingly broad span of legal issues that need to be addressed centrally.

10

THE WAY FORWARD

"It eluded us then, but that's no
matter—tomorrow we will run faster,
stretch out our arms farther . . . "
—F SCOTT FITZGERALD,
The Great Gatsby, Ch 9

The fundamental issues

10.1. Each of the recommendations in Chapter 11 is a piece of a very large jigsaw, whose essential purpose is to help ensure that mentally disordered offenders are cared for and treated by the health and social services and not drawn unnecessarily into the criminal justice system.

10.2. The planning and development of services must reflect the guiding principles of the review, which, as set out at paragraph 3.3, are that patients should be cared for:

- **with regard to the quality of care and proper attention to the needs of individuals;**

- *as far as possible, in the community, rather than in institutional settings;*

- *under conditions of no greater security than is justified by the degree of danger they present to themselves or to others;*

- *in such a way as to maximise rehabilitation and their chances of sustaining an independent life;*

- *as near as possible to their own homes or families if they have them.*

We see the fundamental issues as being:

- **a positive approach to individual needs**

a positive approach to the needs of individual patients, many of whom, including women and people from ethnic minorities, may have special or differing needs;

- **joint working**

a flexible multi-agency and multi-professional approach whose aim is to identify and meet most effectively the needs of mentally disordered offenders;

- *the complementary role of mainstream and specialised services*

the role of general mental health and learning disability services, with access to more specialised services, in providing care and treatment for most mentally disordered offenders;

- **the police**

closer working between the police, health and social services to avoid unnecessary prosecution of mentally disordered suspects;

- **the probation service**

the development of the probation service to:
>   facilitate effective co-operation at local level between criminal justice agencies and health and social services;
>   ensure that prosecutions are not initiated where they could be avoided; and
>   to help divert from custodial disposals mentally disordered people who have to be prosecuted;

- **community care**

an improved range of community care services, including accommodation and day services that are suitable as alternatives to prosecution and will meet the needs of homeless mentally disordered offenders;

- **secure and associated services**

the expansion of medium secure and associated "outreach" services, including in particular those to cater for people with learning disabilities and longer-term medium security needs;

- **health care for prisoners**

the improvement of mental health services for prisoners, to be contracted in mainly from the NHS;

- **the academic and research base**

a stronger academic and research base to underpin service improvements and the general and specialised forensic training of staff to work with mentally disordered offenders.

Evidence of progress

10.3. There is widespread evidence of a more positive approach by a number of agencies to services in this area. This includes specific follow-up to Circular 66/90 (as shown, for example, by the growth in diversion schemes) and other joint initiatives (such as policy agreements and practice guidelines established at both strategic and working levels, as well as locally organised multi-agency conferences to stimulate awareness and co-ordinated action).

10.4. There is also a growing range of innovative service developments and, to judge by visits and responses to our earlier reports, much enthusiasm and interest. This progress is greatly welcomed, but it represents only a start—taken nationally, a fairly modest start—which needs to be nurtured and supported from the top. In this respect, the responses to the recent needs assessment exercise have been valuable in pointing to those parts of the country where agencies are acting positively and in concert and those where they are doing so more haphazardly or, compared to others, less effectively.

10.5. We welcome the sponsorship by the Home Office of a forthcoming series of high-level conferences for health and social services in every Region (including Wales)*. These events, which are being organised by the Mental Health Foundation, should help to raise further the profile of mentally disordered offenders and seek to stimulate, as an adjunct to formal action that may stem from this review, the multi-agency approach.

Joint working nationally and locally

10.6. At the national level, the review itself has contributed to a closer working relationship between the Department of Health and the Home Office. We welcome Ministers' commitment to continue this beyond the review (House of Commons written answers, 13 Nov 1992 and 2 June 1992), but we believe strongly that it requires a continuing formal framework to ensure that awareness of the needs of mentally disordered offenders is sustained and translated into action (OV 32)†.

10.7. The new *Criminal Justice Consultative Council* and the area committees established in the light of the Woolf report will in future provide multi-agency foci for the criminal justice system. These bodies are not designed to provide the focus for health and social services for mentally disordered offenders, although they have an important role in play in some areas (such as health care for prisoners).

* The first conference in this series was held in Oxford Region on 13-14 November 1992. Others will take place in 1993.
† See Foreword to this report.

10.8. Comparable arrangements are needed for mentally disordered offenders. This requires the active participation of all the local agencies concerned, guided and monitored at Regional and national levels. We have already suggested the appointment of consultant advisers in forensic psychiatry as one possible contribution to ensuring that Regional Health Authorities have access to clearly identified sources of advice.

The Health of the Nation White Paper

10.9. We welcome the priority accorded to mentally disordered offenders in the *Health of the Nation* (1992, *op cit*):

> The essential task here is to ensure that mentally disordered offenders who need specialist health and social care are diverted from the criminal justice system as early as possible. This requires close co-operation between all the local agencies concerned. **Authorities' strategic and purchasing plans should include the necessary range of health and social services (both secure and non-secure) to enable them to respond to people's special needs.**

10.10. This is the essential complement to the diversion and discontinuance arrangements promoted in Circular 66/90 and could be matched on the social services side by implementation of our recommendation that services for mentally disordered offenders should form part of local authorities' community care plans for 1993-94.

Effective follow-up of the review

10.11. We think that effective follow-up of this review will require an action plan which sets out clearly the key tasks to be performed and the times by which they are to be achieved. This will need the active involvement of the NHS Management Executive and the Social Services Inspectorate which have formal monitoring responsibilities for health and social services authorities, as well as that of Regional Health Authorities, which have their own monitoring and strategic function. With regard to the criminal justice system, the Home Office would need to spearhead work with the probation, police, and prison services and the courts. Other Departments, including the Lord Chancellor's Department, the Department of the Environment and the Department for Education, may also need to be involved.

10.12. The implementation programme must need be co-ordinated with the work of the recently formed mental illness task force (see paragraph 5.18), bearing in mind particularly that we expect most mentally disordered offenders to be cared for and treated within mainstream services.

10.13. It is vital that the medium secure programme is firmly managed and monitored. In this respect we recognise that the monitoring arrangements that the Department of Health now has in place are far more sophisticated than existed in the mid 1970s. The increased capital for medium secure services in the current financial year is an important step, but there is a need for further medium secure places above the current target of 1,000 and a requirement for more local secure places in lower security.

Continuing work

10.14. We have already identified continuing work on the implications of the review for high security services and on the needs of people with psychopathic disorder. Another key issue is the way that services respond to the needs of people from ethnic minorities. We hope that our discussion paper, with its recommendations, will provide a helpful reference point. There is a need for policy development of the range of special needs issues that have also been the subject of discussion papers and in particular to stimulate services for people with learning disabilities who come within the scope of the review.

10.15. Better information and performance indicators will be needed. The performance management group (see paragraph 8.18) will be looking at these matters.

The next steps

10.16. In many areas, the development of effective diversion arrangements and complementary services for mentally disordered offenders will be starting from a narrow base (CR 4.26). We envisage the developmental process having the following fundamental stages:

   i. *the agreement of a local framework for inter-agency co-operation.* Unless this is in place, services are likely to develop haphazardly, if at all, and will almost certainly fail a number of users;

   ii. *a local assessment of need.* This process has begun, but must be broadened to include all health and social services with need, identified on a multi-agency basis;

iii.   a. *the inclusion of multi-agency plans for mentally disordered offenders in purchasing, service development and other strategies;*

    b. *early action taken centrally, and by local agencies, to determine training requirements and to ensure the development of an adequate academic and research base.* This is a prerequisite for achieving the necessary service changes and ensuring that they lead to real health and social service gains for patients;

iv.   a. *the development of a more effective range and level of health and social services,* a process which includes the contracting in of mental health care to prisons and must move on a broad front in tandem with:

    b. *the development of effective arrangements for:*

the identification of mentally disordered people by the police and their obtaining advice from the health and social services as to suitable care and treatment;

diverting mentally disordered offenders to health and social services care at the pre-court stage. We favour the earliest possible development of assessment and diversion schemes to achieve nationwide coverage;

the identification by the prison service of mentally disordered prisoners who require health or social services care and their transfer to suitable placements.

And finally . . .

10.17. What happens from now on is subject to the decisions and efforts of others. In 1990 we were offered what the then Parliamentary Secretary for Health described as "an excellent opportunity". As we said in our earlier *Overview,* it was one we have welcomed and which we have endeavoured to seize effectively. It has been a great encouragement to us that those who have commented on our reports have very largely endorsed the broad direction we have proposed and our vision of a much more diverse and sensitive range of services, predominantly non-institutional and non-custodial, which effectively and promptly meets individual needs. Fortunately there seems to be widespread agreement about what needs to be done—in itself a helpful base from which to move forward.

10.18. Mentally disordered offenders and others requiring similar services are a vulnerable and, as we have said, too often neglected group of people. Justice for them, as well as our wider interests as a society, demand a more effective response than in the past. We hope that our work has helped to build the foundation on which that response can be given.

11

THE RECOMMENDATIONS

The recommendations made by the various advisory and working groups are listed as follows:

Recommendations are recorded as they appeared in the respective reports, except in a few instances where the wording has been amended very slightly for the sake of clarity. Some recommendations were carried forward or amplified (in a very few instances, effectively amended) as a result of later work; where necessary, cross-references or a supplementary note are provided. A few recommendations largely duplicated each other; again, there are cross-references.

Cross-references to paragraphs in this final report are identified by the prefix, FR.

We identified the issues that we see as fundamental to the effective planning and development of services at paragraph 10.2 above.

Report of the community advisory group

11.1. In line with current policy, mentally disordered offenders should, wherever possible, receive care and treatment from health or social services rather than in the criminal justice system (CR 2.12).

Diversion and discontinuance

11.2. There should be effective local agreements between the police and health, social and probation services as to flexible arrangements for the urgent assessment of people who appear to be mentally disordered. These should include a policy on the use of section 136 of the Mental Health Act 1983 and seek to ensure that, wherever possible, mentally disordered people can receive supportive care without first being taken to a police station as a place of safety. The adequacy of existing agreements should be reviewed (2.10; 2.12). *See also 11.121.*

11.3. Wherever possible, the probation service should be involved before a mentally disordered person has been charged with an offence (2.15).

11.4. There should be closer links between forensic medical examiners (police surgeons) and local psychiatric services to ensure that the needs of mentally disordered people detained in police custody are addressed with urgency and that forensic examiners are encouraged to develop a better understanding of the needs of mentally disordered offenders. We suggest that the establishment of specialist panels may assist forensic examiners to acquire relevant experience (2.18).

11.5. Wherever possible, a mentally disordered person should be assessed by a qualified psychiatrist who is able, where necessary, to provide medical reports for the Crown Prosecution Service and the court and to arrange admission to hospital if this is required in the interests of the person's mental health (2.17-2.18).

11.6. Specialised bail hostels should be developed for some mentally disordered offenders who might otherwise have to be remanded unnecessarily in custody. These hostels would need to develop links with other services to which bailees may require access (2.21). *See also 11.69.*

11.7. There should be an accelerated expansion of bail information schemes (2.22). *See 11.66.*

11.8. There should be an extension in the use of "public interest" case assessment (2.24).

11.9. Pre-court assessments should take account of a mentally disordered person's fitness to plead and ability to cope with a court appearance. Advice should also be offered to the court on suitable disposals (2.26).

11.10. There should be nationwide provision of court psychiatrist or similar schemes for assessment and diversion of mentally disordered offenders. These should be based on a clear local understanding as to the contribution of each agency and where the lead responsibility lies. The finance advisory group should consider the funding arrangements for such schemes and (together with the staffing and training group) the resource implications for health and social services (2.17-2.31). *See also 11.120; 11.207-210; 11.263.*

Community services

11.11. The planning and development of community services for mentally disordered offenders should reflect the criteria at FR 3.3 (3.2).

11.12. Services for mentally disordered offenders should be planned and developed as part of community mental health services generally, but there should be access, if neccessary, to specialised services, including those that take account of a person's offending or special needs. (3.7-3.8).

11.13. Decisions about the level and pattern of general mental illness services should take account of the needs, and access to services, of mentally disordered offenders (3.8). *See also 11.202.*

11.14. Service provision should be tailored to the individual needs of patients and related to the availability and efficient use of resources (3.8).

11.15. There should be active links between community services and those provided in hospitals (including Special Hospitals) and prisons, and steps taken as part of this process to help smooth the transfer of in-patients and prisoners to community care (3.12).

11.16. The "care programme" approach applies not only to patients discharged from hospitals, but also to those leaving prison or referred to the specialised psychiatric services from elsewhere in the criminal justice system. This needs to be publicised better among the agencies concerned, as does the potential contribution of these agencies to the success of care programmes (3.15). *See also 11.87; 11.93; 11.116; 11.211-213; 11.272.*

11.17. The possible use of probation orders with a condition of psychiatric treatment should be considered more frequently (3.19).

11.18. When considering the accommodation needs of a mentally disordered offender, the possible need for additional health and social services support, including day services, should be taken into account (3.22).

11.19. Agencies concerned with mentally disordered offenders should develop collaborative arrangements designed to ensure a co-ordinated approach to service provision and overcome problems arising from the absence of common boundaries. We think that these arrangements will need a Regional or supra-district focus, although they should take account also of mental health services provided locally. They will need to develop effective working arrangements (or possibly be combined with) local committees bringing together elements of the criminal justice system that may be established in the light of the Woolf report (Cm 1456) (3.24-3.33). *See also 11.125.*

11.20. There should be core teams of professional staff responsible for ensuring that mentally disordered offenders in a particular area are properly assessed and receive (mostly through general mental illness teams) the continuing care and treatment they need in the right kind of setting. The operation of an individual care programme is likely to be enhanced by the appointment of a care co-ordinator from within the core team or the general mental illness team (3.34-3.36). *See also FR 4.11-12 and 11.201-204.*

11.21. The staffing and training advisory group should consider the roles of social workers and probation officers in the assessment and care of mentally disordered offenders (3.38). *See 11.164-168; 11.191-196.*

11.22. The organisation of health and social services should reflect the possibility that mentally disordered offenders may need access to them at any time of day or night (3.41-42). *(The staffing and training advisory group reconsidered a further part of this recommendation that there should be a "single and consistent" inter-agency referral point, ideally based within a central resource centre, to act as a focus for entry to such services or to assist in arranging assessments or referrals within the services: 11.217).*

11.23. Community services, drawing where necessary on the outreach services provided from more centralised facilities, should seek to respond locally to a wide a range of individual needs as possible. There should be no automatic presumption of passing on to a supra-district or Regional service those with specialised needs (3.46).

11.24. Placements outside the district, including those in independent facilities, should form part of the planned provision of a comprehensive local service with effective community links (3.46). *See 11.272.*

11.25. Contracting and other arrangements developed locally for provision for mentally disordered offenders must operate in the interests of patient care and service to secure the contributions of the various agencies. Agencies should be aware of the groundrules on patients' residence to which others are working and should work together to ensure that patients are not denied services through boundary or other bureaucratic disputes (3.33; 3.48).

Families, carers and users

11.26. Families and carers should, wherever practicable, be regarded as part of the team responsible for a patient and their own needs taken into account (3.44; FR 4.17). *See also 11.87 and 11.123.*

11.27. Service users should, wherever possible, be involved in care and treatment decisions and their views taken into account in service planning (3.45).

Strategic issues

11.28. The research advisory group should consider whether a national study of need for community services for mentally disordered offenders should be commissioned (4.5). *See FR 7.10 and figure 9.*

11.29. There should be local multi-agency assessments of need for community services for mentally disordered offenders. Service provision thereafter should reflect continuing needs assessment and evaluation (4.7; 4.10).

11.30. A range of indicators should be developed to measure the quality and effectiveness of care provided for mentally disordered offenders (4.13). *See 11.270.*

11.31. Government guidance with implications for services for mentally disordered offenders should be drawn to the attention of all agencies with a likely interest in its contents (4.16).

11.32. Consideration should be given to extending the broad effect of the "Malone-Lee" letter of 28 September 1990 (NHS Management Executive Letter (90190) beyond the end of 1991, taking account as necessary of proposals emerging from this review and the developing "purchaser/provider" arrangements in the NHS (4.18). *This has been implemented: FR 2.13–14.*

11.33. The Steering Committee should consider the need for arrangements at national level to provide a continuing overview across the range of health and social services for mentally disordered offenders. This should take account of the contribution of associated agencies (4.20). *See also 11.49 and FR 10.6.*

11.34. The finance advisory group should consider the scope for earmarking financial resources for services for mentally disordered offenders in ways that do not inhibit local initiative (4.22). *See 11.253.*

11.35. *The community advisory group recommended that all relevant agencies, working together, should give priority to a series of service development tasks (CR 4.25). This recommendation has been subsumed in FR 10.1–2 and 10.16.*

Report of the hospital advisory group

Strategic and managerial issues

11.36. We fully endorse the Government's policy that all required psychiatric services, including in-patient provision for difficult to manage patients and mentally disordered offenders, must be re-provided before existing mental illness or mental handicap hospitals are vacated (2.13).

11.37. Regular (probably annual) monitoring should be undertaken by the Department of Health, which should identify the capacity of Special Hospitals, NHS secure provision at all levels and secure capacity in independent mental nursing homes (2.17).

11.38. The staffing and training advisory group should consider the training needs of those in the criminal justice system who deal with mentally disordered offenders: (3.7). *See 11.197–199.*

11.39. The finance advisory group should examine how the development of services for mentally disordered offenders can be ensured under the purchaser/provider arrangements or whether any refinements of the general arrangements would be needed (4.4). *See finance group recommendations at 11.245 et seq.*

11.40. *The hospital advisory group recommended (FR 4.8) that each Health Region should have one or more service development teams guided by a forensic psychiatric adviser to assist in the development and monitoring of forensic psychiatric services and secure hospital provision. The appointment of a forensic adviser is considered as an option at FR 4.9 which emphasises both the importance of the Regional role and of high quality advice on mentally disordered offender services being available to Regional Health Authorities.*

11.41. Each health authority (probably through arrangements at Regional or supra-district level) should be responsible for the development and operation of the NHS contribution to screening, assessment and diversion schemes in courts, police stations and prisons within its catchment area regardless of where the individuals requiring assessment are considered to reside. This must include a responsibility to ensure that patients are admitted for assessment and/or treatment as soon as is clinically required (4.11). *See below.*

11.42. The financial implications of 11.41 should be considered by the finance advisory group (4.13). *See 11.250–252.*

11.43. The staffing and training advisory group should consider the role of the probation service in the provision of social work to mentally disordered offenders, including training for probation officers in relevant aspects of mental health legislation (4.17). *See 11.166–168; 11.191–196.*

11.44. We strongly endorse efforts being made to achieve an appropriate allocation of resources to allow Social Services Departments to provide health-related social work for patients who originate from outside their catchment areas (4.22).

11.45. It should remain the responsibility of Social Services Departments to provide an adequate level of support to hospitals and units which deal with mentally disordered offenders, but hospitals should employ social workers directly if the required level of service cannot be achieved otherwise (4.25). *Cf 11.162 and 11.169.*

11.46. The finance advisory group should consider how to increase the flexibility of finances both between Social Services Departments, and between Social Services Departments, the NHS and the probation service, including the role of the mental illness specific grant. Thus, for example, Social Services Departments might be able to charge each other for services to people from other parts of the country. Health Authorities or Hospitals might be able to assist in paying for social workers where there is disagreement between the two agencies about the appropriate level of social work support (4.27). *See finance group recommendations at 11.245 et seq.*

11.47. Professional staff from health, social and probation services (and others if necessary) should attend regular case conferences for each patient from their area who is in a Special Hospital and that they should be involved in the admissions process, and in assessing the treatment and, as necessary, continuing care needs of their residents who are in Special Hospital (4.30).

11.48. The finance advisory group should consider how best to remove perverse financial incentives to ensure that levels of care and security are not influenced by changes of funding agency (4.32). *See finance group recommendations at 11.245 et seq.*

11.49. A permanent national focus should be established for agencies involved with mentally disordered offenders (5.3). *See also 11.33 and FR 10.6. An advisory committee on mentally disordered offenders is being established for a period of three years: see Foreword.*

11.50. Regular monitoring should be carried out not only of actual movements of mentally disordered offenders from the criminal justice system to hospital (as is the case at present), but also of cases where clinicians felt that such a transfer should be made and no place was forthcoming (5.6).

11.51. The number of professional staff with training in forensic psychiatry should be increased to take account of recommendations by the various advisory groups; work to identify the scale of the increase should be initiated as soon as possible; and planning by the Department of Health and the Home Office should take into account of the financial and other implications of the hospital advisory group's recommendations (7.5). *See staffing and training recommendations at 11.147 et seq.*

Levels of hospital provision

11.52. Regional Health Authorities should (in conjunction with other relevant agencies) ensure that there is a regular assessment of the needs of their residents for secure provision and of the non-secure hospital needs of mentally disordered offenders updated annually (5.10). *See below.*

11.53. The above process should start as soon as possible so that regional health authorities produce their first assessment of needs before the end of this review (5.11). *See FR 4.5–7.*

11.54. In order to assist with needs assessment, information about mentally disordered offenders in prisons and Special Hospitals should be regularly disseminated to each Regional Health Authority (5.14).

11.55. The capacity of Special Hospitals should be maintained for the time being at around 1,700 places, but should be kept under regular review. Further consideration should be given to the proximity of Special Hospital provision to the populations it serves (5.23). *See FR 5.26–7.*

11.56. Adequate funding should be provided to support the urgent implementation of current plans for additional medium secure places, pending the adoption of the new targets we recommend at paragraph 11.59 *(and now 11.274)* (5.25).

11.57. The needs of all patients who require treatment in conditions of medium security should be considered as part of the medium secure programme. This may include discrete units or units integrated with general psychiatric provision where this is clinically required. Furthermore, existing secure provision for those with special needs should be protected, at least until there is an alternative way of meeting such needs (5.29). *See Annex B.*

11.58. Medium secure facilities should be available for those patients who require them, irrespective of the length of stay they require (5.33).

11.59. *The hospital advisory group recommended that the number of medium secure places should be increased (HR 5.36). It considered that, in the light of the recommendation at paragraph 11.57 and from information already available, at least 1,500 medium secure places would be required nationally. It further recommended that revised Regional targets should be established during the course of the review, once the results of urgent needs assessment were known, and kept under review in the light of subsequent assessments. This recommendation has been reformulated (as at 11.274) in the light of developments: see FR 5.19—5.25.*

11.60. Every district health authority should, in line with existing Government policy, ensure the availability of secure provision for patients with mental illness or learning disabilities. This should include provision for intensive care as well as for those who require long term treatment and/or care (5.37). *See also 11.115 and 11.127.*

Quality of life

11.61. Examples of good practice in the design and operation of secure hospital provision should be regularly collated and disseminated to relevant professionals (6.8).

11.62. A comprehensive system of clinical audit should be developed as an integral part of audit generally, by the appropriate medical, nursing and social services organisations. This system should operate in all hospitals where psychiatric patients are detained under the Mental Health Act, including Special Hospitals, NHS hospitals (including NHS Trusts) and independent sector hospitals (6.12).

Psychopathic disorder

11.63. Urgent evaluation and research should be carried out to establish a basis for the future development of health and social services for people with psychopathic disorder (7.15). *See FR 1.22-23.*

Report of the prison advisory group

Diversion and transfer from prison

11.64. The powers that enable remands to prison for the primary purpose of medical assessment in the Bail Act 1976 and the Magistrates' Court Act 1980 should be reviewed with a view to amendment or repeal (PR 3.3). *See also FR 9.6 and 11.276.*

11.65. Prison medical staff and probation officers should be made more aware of the options for diversion to the care of health and social services in the community and the need to identify those who might benefit from them to the courts at the earliest possible opportunity (3.4).

11.66. Bail information schemes should be extended to all probation areas (3.5). *See also 11.7.*

11.67. Close links should be developed between the medical support provided for specialised bail hostels and prison medical staff (3.6). *See also 11.6.*

11.68. The Health Care Service for Prisoners should ensure that all prisoners in whom there is evidence of mental disorder and/or are awaiting disposal under the Mental Health Act 1983 are assessed immediately on arrival at prison reception. All other prisoners should be assessed for mental disorder within 24 hours of admission (3.10).

11.69. The Health Care Service for Prisoners should make greater use of transfers under section 48 of the Mental Health Act 1983. (The Health Care Service recommends section 48 transfers in all cases where a doctor would recommend in-patient treatment for the patient concerned if he or she were seen at an out-patient clinic in the community.) Section 48 should be reviewed with the aim of widening its scope to provide similar provision for transfer to hospital to those set out in section 47, and to include all Mental Health Act disorders (3.11). *See also FR 9.6 and 11.276.*

11.70. Urgent requests for transfer assessments should be carried out as soon as practicable and in any event within 72 hours of the request being made. Health Authorities should aim to assess 50 per cent of cases within seven days of referral by the Health Care Service for Prisoners and 90 per cent within 14 days (3.13).

11.71. All prison doctors should have a list of the Regional forensic advisers *[or the equivalent]*, who should be approached if there is any doubt as to which hospital should be asked to undertake any assessment of a prisoner (3.14).

11.72. The managing medical officer at each prison should negotiate with the Governor for greater flexibility in arranging assessments by outside consultants. An appropriate room should be provided at each prison for psychiatric assessments. All medical information about prisoners should be made available to visiting psychiatrists (3.16).

11.73. The responsible medical officers should be required to submit regular progress reports to the patient's previous prison medical officer and the Health Care Service for Prisoners should give early warnings of any intention to remit to prison (3.19).

Raising the profile of prisoners with mental health care needs

11.74. There should be a clear statement of policy, complementary to the existing policy on diversion, in relation to the care and treatment of prisoners with mental health care needs. This statement should cover the role of the mental health care services in the identification and assessment of mental disorder, crisis intervention, and continuing treatment on the basis of individual care plans for those for whom transfer from prison is either not possible or delayed (4.3).

11.75. The research advisory group should consider the need for research designed to inform the development of policy in relation to the care of prisoners with mental health care needs (4.4). *See figure 9.*

11.76. In addition to the policy statement recommended at 11.74, all prison Governors should have responsibility for ensuring that provision for those with mental health care needs is included in their contracts with Area Managers (4.6).

11.77. *The prison advisory group supported the intention of the then Directorate of Prison Medical Services Standards Working Group to prescribe standards by the end of 1991 for health care aspects of prison reception arrangements and suggested that these should include specific standards related to mental health care screening (4.9). See also 11.95.*

11.78. The Health Advisory Committee on prison health care should be invited to give early priority to consideration of the conclusions which emerge from this review (4.10).

11.79. Improving co-operation between agencies (statutory and non-statutory) is of such importance that it can properly be regarded as an objective in its own right. A common approach to assessing value for money and monitoring performance from agencies responsible for contributing resources would be a useful starting point (4.13).

Prison services

11.80. We support the plans to extend the experience learned from Grendon Prison in providing for difficult prisoners to a further establishment or prison units (5.6).

11.81. Staffing levels of the Wormwood Scrubs Hospital Annexe should be maintained (5.11).

11.82. The Department of Health should consider the need for guidance to NHS staff on co-operation with prisons on suicide prevention. Consultant psychiatrists should be co-opted as members of Suicide Prevention Management Groups in local prisons, and prisons with specialised facilities (5.22). *See also 11.105-106; 11.160.*

11.83. The Department of Health, the Home Office and other relevant bodies should establish a working group to review the treatment options for people with personality (psychopathic) disorders, their appropriate location and the arrangements for placing offenders in need of treatment (5.24). *See also 11.63 and FR 1.22-23.*

11.84. We strongly support the proposal of the joint Home Office/Department of Health Scrutiny Implementation Working Party that the Prison Service should contract in a specialised mental health care service, initially for remand prisoners. We also endorse the proposal that the Health Care Service for Prisoners should take up with the appropriate professional bodies the question of accrediting post for the purposes of providing recognised training in psychiatry (5.30) *See also FR 5.31-33 and 11.96; ST 4.17 (on accreditation).*

11.85. The Home Office, the Department of Health and the Special Hospitals Service Authority should explore together the best way forward in developing links between the special Hospitals and the specialist prison facilities holding dangerous mentally disordered offenders (5.31). *See FR 5.26-7.*

11.86. The issue of the confidentiality of records relating to prisoners with mental health problems should be referred to the staffing and training advisory group (5.32). *See 11.206.*

11.87. Discharge planning should involve the specialised mental health care team and others (such as the housing, education, employment and social security services) who will be responsible for providing services for a former prisoner in the community or in hospital. Wherever possible, prisoners and their families should be involved in the planning process (5.36). *See also 11.16; 11.211-212.*

Report of the official working group on services for people with special needs

11.88. Agencies' approach to services for mentally disordered offenders with special needs should be consistent with the considerations at FR 3.9 (SN 2.2).

11.89. The planning of services for mentally disordered offenders, based on local needs assessments, and the wider links developed by specialised teams dealing with such patients, should take particular account of the additional inputs that may be required to identify and provide for special needs at key points of the system (2.6).

11.90. Wherever possible, the special needs of mentally disordered offenders should be met by local services, but where, in the best interests of the patient, it is necessary to make referrals to services outside the locality, effective links should be maintained with those in a patient's home district (2.8). *See also 11.23.*

11.91. The finance advisory group should consider the implications of "purchaser/provider" arrangements for services with an extra-Regional catchment, including the need for effective mechanisms to ensure that, where necessary, specialised services for mentally disordered offenders can be developed and maintained supra-Regionally (2.15). *See 11.261.*

11.92. In suitable cases, supra-Regional funding should be regarded as a realistic option for health services for mentally disordered offenders with a supra-Regional or national catchment (2.15).

11.93. Staff from other health and social service teams should, as necessary, be involved with the mental health care services in the operation of care programmes or other continuing care arrangements for mentally disordered offenders with special needs. These arrangements should take account of any special requirements, including therapy needs, that patients may have to enable them to contribute to decisions about future care (2.37). *See also 11.201.*

11.94. Agencies should ensure that staff are trained in the recognition and initial handling of a broad range of special needs (2.39).

Health care for prisoners (SN 2.29)

11.95. Specific standards relating to mental health care screening on reception to prison should take account of the importance of identifying special needs.

11.96. Contracts for the delivery of mental health care services to prisons should include a requirement for staff to facilitate, as necessary, arrangements to meet the additional special needs of patients.

Brain injury (SN 4.2)

11.97. Greater awareness of brain injury should be encouraged among the police and other criminal justice staff.

11.98. Effective links should be developed between brain injury services and other services dealing with mentally disordered offenders.

11.99. The particular needs of offenders with brain injury should be recognised in agencies' planning, including the need for access to specialised rehabilitation services and for a positive and co-ordinated approach (involving families, carers and employers as necessary) to rehabilitation in the community.

Hearing impairment (SN 4.5)

11.100. Strategies for mentally disordered offenders should take account of the need for staff in a range of settings to be able to recognise and respond to the needs of deaf or hearing impaired people. There should be access to interpreters and speech therapists (including, where necessary, in police stations and courts) and a positive approach to screening. Imaginative programmes should be developed for profoundly deaf people who may, in some instances, require access to specialised services away from (but with continuing links with) their home district.

Substance misuse (SN 4.8)

11.101. Active links should be developed between services for mentally disordered offenders and those for substance misusers, including strategic co-ordination between multi-agency groups for mentally disordered offenders, area committees for the criminal justice system and Regional co-ordinative systems for alcohol and drug misuse services.

Sex offenders with mental health care needs (SN 4.10)

11.102. The Department of Health and the Home Office should consider issuing multi-disciplinary guidance on the treatment and supervision of sex offenders to the NHS and probation and social services.

11.103. The Department of Health and the Home Office should give further consideration to the implications for sex offenders of the Efficiency Scrutiny of the Prison Medical Service (now the Health Care Service for Prisoners).

11.104. The Department of Health and the Home Office should follow closely the work of the National Association for the Development of Work with Sex Offenders.

Suicide prevention (SN 4.13)

11.105. A range of health and personal social service staff should be involved in prison Suicide Prevention Management Groups. *See also 11.160.*

11.106. The Department of Health should consider the need for more broadly-based guidance for health and social services staff on suicide prevention, including advice on the effective application of care programmes. *See 11.82, which this recommendation extends.*

11.107. Indicators should be developed which can help to measure the effectiveness of services in minimising suicide and self-harm among mentally disordered people. *(See The Health of the Nation (Cm 1986), Section C.)*

Children and adolescents (SN 4.20)

11.108. There should be research to establish the national prevalence of children and adolescents requiring secure or related specialised services.

11.109. Current levels of secure health provision for mentally disordered adolescents should at least be maintained, preferably through closer links with services provided by other agencies.

11.110. Regional Health Authorities, in conjunction with other agencies, should consider establishing small core teams which can provide advice and support to those caring for mentally disordered children and adolescents with specialised needs.

11.111. As far as possible, specialised services for mentally disordered adolescents should be developed as part of a wider multi-agency service that incorporates provision in a range of settings. *See also 11.124.*

Elderly people (SN 4.21)

11.112. Special consideration should be given to elderly mentally disordered offenders to ensure that their physical, sensory and mental health needs are properly identified and that placements, support services and continuing care arrangements generally can meet these effectively.

Women (SN 4.23)

11.113. Agencies should examine the range of care and support available to female mentally disordered offenders to ensure that services, including staffing and training policies, are capable of being properly responsive to the individual needs and aspirations of women. *See also 11.200.*

11.114. Agencies should ensure that a range of suitable accommodation is available so that female mentally disordered defendants are not remanded unnecessarily in custody.

Official working group report on services for people with learning disabilities or with autism

11.115. Suitable provision for people with learning disabilities, based on assessments of need, should be recognised explicitly as an aim of the medium secure programme (SN 2.22). *See also 11.57.*

11.116. The care programme arrangements should apply explicitly to offenders with learning disabilities leaving hospital or prison who need continuing care from the health and social services. The education services should, as necessary, be involved in such arrangements (SN 2.39). *See also 11.87.*

11.117. Staff in a range of agencies (particularly non-clinical staff) who come into contact with mentally disordered offenders should be trained to understand and, if possible, recognise the particular characteristics and needs of people with learning disabilities. They should also be able to distinguish between learning disabilities and mental illness (LD 2.8). *See also 11.197-199.*

11.118. Definitive central guidance should be issued on the provision of services for offenders with learning disabilities and others requiring similar services. This should be brought to the attention of all relevant services, including criminal justice, education and housing agencies. It should take account of recommendations emerging from this review and the parallel group looking at services for people with learning disabilities and severe psychiatric or behavioural disturbance *(FR 3.11)*, as well as requirements set out in earlier guidance (3.1).

11.119. Local agencies should consider jointly practical ways of raising the service profile of offenders with learning disabilities (3.38).

11.120. Court diversion and assessment schemes should develop effective links with local learning disability teams and, where possible, team members should be encouraged to contribute to schemes, possibly on a rota basis (4.11).

11.121. Local agreements on the operation of section 136 of the Mental Health Act 1983 should give special consideration to the particular needs of people with learning disabilities (4.11). *See also 11.2.*

11.122. At the very least, there should be a re-statement to health authorities that no Special Hospital patient requiring a transfer to a Regional or district facility should have to wait for more than a year. Transfers should normally be effected much more speedily than this. *(This should apply equally to mentally ill patients, who were covered by a similar requirement in Health Circular (88)43, and those with psychopathic disorder)* (4.19).

11.123. Agencies working with children with learning disabilities/difficulties should develop a co-ordinated range of specialised services, sensitive to the wishes of parents and children alike, to meet in the round the needs of those who develop behavioural difficulties (5.16).

11.124. Agencies should develop a joint approach to ensuring that adolescents with learning disabilities who offend or appear to be at risk of offending have access to a range of general and specialised services suitable for their age and stage of development and that they do not get drawn unnecessarily into the criminal justice system (5.22).

11.125. Local multi-agency groups for mentally disordered offender services and area committees for the criminal justice system should provide a clear focus for, or maintain effective links with, relevant services for people with learning disabilities (6.1).

11.126. Future needs assessments (carrying forward work done in the light of NHS Management Executive Letter (92)24 and undertaken on a multi-agency basis) should give more specific attention to the needs of people with learning disabilities (6.4). *See FR 5.22.*

11.127. Regional targets for medium secure beds should include a learning disability element specifically identified and related to a wider Regional strategy (6.9). *See also 11.274.*

11.128. The Department of Health should issue practical guidance on the development of medium secure provision for people with learning disabilities (6.9).

11.129. Agencies should develop joint plans to identify and provide for the specific needs of people with mild to moderate learning disabilities, including in particular those who offend or are at risk of offending (6.13).

11.130. In planning services for, and delivering services to, offenders with learning disabilities, agencies should jointly take account of individuals' longer-term needs, including the social, clinical, educational and resource implications of failing to respond effectively (7.4).

11.131. Effective links should be maintained or developed between learning disability, general psychiatric, forensic pysychiatric and child and adolescent psychiatric services. There may be scope for joint consultant appointments covering more than one of these specialities (7.15). *See also 11.223.*

11.132. As part of the re-examination of training targets for nursing staff proposed at 11.180, health authorities should consider the particular requirement for skilled nurses to work with offenders with learning disabilities and others requiring similar services. They should address also the ways in which forensic psychiatric, general psychiatric and mental handicap nursing relate to each other (7.19).

11.133. The development of a core therapy service for mentally disordered offenders, as proposed at 11.163, should take account of the needs of offenders with learning disabilities and others with similar needs (7.29).

11.134. Having regard to the overall framework of research on services for mentally disordered offenders, priority for research on learning disabilities should be given to the areas identified at LD 8.2 (8.5). *See also FR 7.10 and 11.137.*

Autism

11.135. Agencies should take account of the specialised and varying needs of offenders with autism, including the importance of links with other services that may be required (9.12).

11.136. Agencies should train their staff to recognise and, where possible, respond to the special challenges that autistic people present (9.12).

11.137. There should be research into the range of responses required to meet the needs of autistic people who offend or who have severe behavioural problems. (9.12).

Discussion paper on services for black and ethnic minority groups (see FR 3.5-6)

11.138. There should be strong proactive equal opportunity policies relating to race and culture established in all agencies involved with mentally disordered offenders. The policies should be known and understood by staff and made widely available. Implementation should be monitored. *See also 11.200.*

11.139. There should be explicit consideration of race and culture in the professional and vocational training of all those working with mentally disordered offenders.

11.140. Early training on a multi-agency basis and linked to service provision should take place with the involvement of ethnic minority groups.

11.141. Organisations involved with services for mentally disordered offenders should review their strategies and policies in the light of issues of race and culture.

11.142. Health and local authorities should enable agencies from black and ethnic minority communities to develop and provide services for mentally disordered offenders.

11.143. Representatives from ethnic minority communities should be involved in the planning, development and monitoring of services for mentally disordered offenders.

11.144. Funding should be made available to establish an action research project on the diversion from custody of people from ethnic minority communities.

11.145. Research priorities should be discussed with members of the various ethnic minority communities and consideration given to their areas of concern.

11.146. A co-ordinated system of ethnicity data collection should be established within all agencies concerned with mentally disordered offenders. *See also 11.205-206.*

Report of the staffing and training advisory group

11.147. The Steering Committee should consider how work on the staffing and training implications of services for mentally disordered offenders with "special needs" can best be carried forward (ST 1.5). *See FR 6.7.*

11.148. Our findings should be used as a basis for initial planning, but the results of objective local needs assessments, together with data obtained in due course from improved information and other systems, should be built into rolling projections of future staffing and training needs (1.12).

11.149. Staffing requirements should be determined locally to reflect the level and pattern of services indicated by needs assessments and quality requirements. They should not be calculated simply as a proportion of broad national estimates (1.2).

11.150. The apparent discrepancies between Department of Health and Royal College of Psychiatrists staffing data should be examined in the interests of seeking consistency in the future (2.3).

11.151. As is already intended, information on the staffing of medium secure units should be collected on a regular and consistent basis (2.4).

11.152. The adequacy of relevant targets for senior registrar and registrar numbers should be considered in light of recommendations made by the current review (2.8).

11.153. Family health service authorities should ensure that their assessments of need and consequent planning of primary care services take account of mentally disordered offenders and the links that will be necessary with other agencies (2.16).

11.154. The Department of Health should consider the need for more comprehensive data on the staffing of social services for mentally disordered offenders (and, where appopriate, general mental illness and learning disability services) (2.37).

Future staffing implications

Medical staff (ST 3.14-36)

11.155. Increases in general adult and forensic consultant psychiatrists should be preceded by an expansion in senior registrar and registrar numbers, matched by increases in other disciplines contributing to multi-disciplinary work.

11.156. As a preliminary to the expansion of consultant posts recommended by the staffing and training advisory group, Regional Health Authorities should fund as soon as possible the unfilled senior registrar posts in forensic and, where appropriate, general psychiatry that have been agreed by the Joint Planning Advisory Committee.

11.157. Consideration should be given by the Department of Health, the Health Care Service for Prisoners, the Royal College of Psychiatrists and the Joint Planning Advisory Committee to our initial estimate that, over the next five to 10 years, some 80 new consultant forensic psychiatrist posts and 175 other consultant posts may be needed to meet the expanding clinical needs of services for mentally disordered offenders. They should consider also what uplift will be necessary to take account of factors such as audit, monitoring, evaluation, training and academic work, as well services for "special needs" groups. *See also 11.225.*

11.158. In conjunction with 11.157, consideration should be given to the number of registrar and senior registrar posts that will be required to ensure that there are sufficiently qualified doctors to fill and, in future years, maintain the increased number of consultant posts.

Prison health care (ST 3.24-31)

11.159. Staff working with mentally disordered offenders (in prison or elsewhere) should be encouraged to report to their managers any problems which hinder their effective delivery of patient care. They should also be able to feel confident that such reports will be taken seriously and that, where necessary and possible, remedial action will be taken.

11.160. Contributions to Suicide Prevention Management Groups should be sought from a range of health, social and probation services staff as a matter of course. *(This supplements the recommendation at 11.82.)*

Nursing

11.161. Employing authorities, in conjunction with schools of nursing, should consider the implications for nurse staffing and training of the proposed increases in medium secure beds. There should also be joint planning between these bodies and local prisons to ensure that the future specialised needs of prisoners can be met (3.42).

Therapists (ST 3.47)

11.162. Medium secure units should have the financial flexibility to purchase therapy services directly if these cannot otherwise be secured. *Cf 11.169.*

11.163. Early priority should be given to expanding therapy services based in Special Hospitals and medium secure units. Agencies generally should give active consideration to the role of therapists working with mentally disordered offenders so that their future involvement in such services can be planned more effectively. *See also 11.133.*

Social and probation services (ST 3.48-61; 3.63-68)

11.164. Services for mentally disordered offenders should form part of local authorities' community care plans for 1993-94.

11.165. Local authorities should consider designating a senior officer to be responsible for the overall development of work with mentally disordered offenders.

11.166. Social and probation services should establish mechanisms for closer working in identifying the accommodation and support needs of mentally disordered offenders.

11.167. Probation officers should be part of mental health care teams contracted in to prisons.

11.168. Consideration should be given to seconding probation officers for work in medium secure units.

Education

11.169. Medium secure units should have the financial flexibility to purchase education services directly if these cannot otherwise be secured (3.72). *Cf 11.162.*

Training and education needs

11.170. Training for work with mentally disordered offenders should be reflected in the plans of all relevant agencies and, as far as possible, these should be based on joint or complementary approaches. Action locally should be matched by a coordinated approach to training issues at national level (4.5).

Medical staff (ST 4.6-23)

11.171. Consultant posts with a special interest in forensic psychiatry should be retained for the time being, but their existence should be kept under review.

11.172. All specialised forensic psychiatric training should include an academic component.

11.173. Forensic psychiatry should be covered in the Royal College of Psychiatrists' forthcoming guidance on the continuing education of consultants.

11.174. Forensic issues should be covered in general psychiatric training for medical students.

11.175. Regional forensic advisers [or the equivalent] should be responsible, in consultation with other forensic psychiatrists, for ensuring that optimum medical training opportunities in forensic settings are available at both basic and post-qualifying levels. See 11.40 and FR 4.9.

11.176. Options for improving effective working between forensic and general psychiatry, and other psychiatric specialties, should be explored and, where possible, developed. See also 11.131 and 11.233.

11.177. An early induction course should be mandatory for doctors working regularly in the Health Care Service for Prisoners. This should be designed to familiarise them with a range of clinical, legal and operational issues.

11.178. Staff grade or consultant psychiatrists involved in work with prisoners should undertake a specialised post-induction course.

11.179. Training opportunities for psychotherapy with mentally disordered offenders should be increased. The development of such training should be based initially on units which currently have psychotherapists working with these or similar patients.

Nursing (ST 4.24–36)

11.180. Health authorities should re-examine their training targets for psychiatric nurses in light of this review. See also 11.132.

11.181. Training courses for community psychiatric nurses should include consideration of forensic nursing issues and opportunities for placements in forensic settings.

11.182. The English National Board (ENB) should consider the future need for Project 2000 training in forensic psychiatric nursing, including opportunities for suitable placements.

11.183. The ENB should continue to encourage the development of joint training schemes between the independent sector and the NHS.

11.184. There should be a speedy introduction of more flexible arrangements for, and content of, post-basic education and training in subjects related to forensic nursing, including greater opportunities for open learning and better links with further and higher education.

11.185. Initiatives taken to enrol prison nurses on specialised ENB courses should be maintained and developed.

11.186. Prisons should continue to forge closer links with local hospitals, colleges of nursing and others who can assist in the development of nurse education.

Psychology

11.187. Employing authorities should give urgent consideration to the need for an increase in post-graduate training places for clinical psychologists to work with mentally disordered offenders (4.39).

Therapists (ST 4.41–48)

11.188. Consideration should be given to the need for specialised post-qualifying training for occupational therapists working in secure settings.

11.189. There should be increased training opportunities for occupational therapy helpers and technical instructors working with mentally disordered offenders to attain professional status and generally to improve their skills.

11.190. The Department of Health and the College of Speech and Language Therapists should give further consideration to the development of an advanced specialised course for speech and language therapists working in psychiatry. They should consider also the scope for encouraging the development of speech and language therapy departments.

Social and probation services (ST 4.49–61)

11.191. The Central Council for Education and Training in Social Work (CCETSW) should provide guidance on the particular skills required by social workers and probation officers involved in the care and management of mentally disordered offenders.

11.192. CCETSW should consider the need for an additional specialised training module which addresses the skills and knowledge needed by social workers and probation officers working with mentally disordered offenders or similar patients in secure settings.

11.193. Post-qualifying education and training should be readily available for social services and probation staff working in a range of settings who are likely to come into contact with mentally disordered offenders.

11.194. Revised guidance on the training and preparation of approved social workers should ensure that there is an adequate emphasis on the particular issues relating to mentally disordered offenders and on the working of the criminal justice system. There should also be training in the supervision provisions of the Criminal Procedure (Insanity and Unfitness to Plead) Act 1991. Practice placements in forensic settings should be encouraged.

11.195. The Social Services Training Support Programme should make provision for the training of staff working with mentally disordered offenders. *See also 11.266.*

11.196. The Department of Health and the Home Office should continue to encourage joint discussions between the probation and social work professions on their developing interface in work with mentally disordered offenders.

Criminal justice services (ST 4.62–69)

11.197. Police training should cover relevant aspects of the Mental Health Act 1983 and the initial identification of suspects who appear to be mentally disordered. There should also be opportunities for "refresher" training and joint training with other groups working with mentally disordered offenders. *See also 11.117.*

11.198. The Home Office and Department of Health should explore with the Lord Chancellor's Department, the Crown Prosecution Service and relevant professional and training bodies how training for court-based and legal staff who come into contact with mentally disordered offenders could best be promoted and made more widely available. *See also 11.117.*

11.199. Effective links should be developed between local Law Societies and multi-agency groups for mentally disordered offenders.

Multi-agency issues

Equal opportunities

11.200. Agencies' staffing and training policies should adopt a positive approach to the special needs of women and people from ethnic minorities (5.7). *See also 11.138–140.*

Multi-professional core teams (ST 5.8–5.12)

11.201. Agencies developing multi-professional core teams *[FR 11.20]* should consider the scope for cross-membership with other relevant teams in the interests of overall service effectiveness. *See also 11.204.*

11.202. The need to care for and treat mentally disordered offenders who are not referred to the specialised forensic (or other specialised) services should be reflected in the staffing and training of general mental health teams. *See also 11.13.*

11.203. There should be closer links between teams caring for mentally disordered offenders and local social security offices to heighten understanding of the benefits system and to help ensure the prompt availability of benefit to those who qualify for it.

11.204. *Core teams should involve the groups listed at FR 4.11. There should be identifiable links with those at FR 4.12.*

Information (ST 5.15-21)

11.205. Comprehensive information on the use of section 136 of the Mental Health Act 1983 should be collected in a standardised form so that satisfactory estimates can be made of the resource (including staffing and accommodation) implications of increased referrals to the health and social services. We support the view of the community advisory group that research is needed on the use of section 136 of the Mental Health Act 1983.

11.206. Consideration should be given to the development of systems which enable information that is likely to be needed, in a patient's interests, by practitioners in a range of agencies to be available across agency boundaries. These might operate under the aegis of strategic multi-agency groups for mentally disordered offenders (possibly linked to area committees for the criminal justice system). Account should be taken of ethical and practical difficulties, as well as any views expressed through consultation on the staffing and training advisory group report.

Court diversion schemes (ST 5.22-29).

11.207. Any national view on preferred models for court-based assessment and diversion schemes should be taken only after the growing range of such schemes, and outcomes for patients, have been fully evaluated.

11.208. Agencies proposing to establish court diversion schemes should work jointly from the outset to secure the range of professional inputs that may be needed and to assess the potential resource (including staffing and training) implications of increased diversion to the health and social services.

11.209. Broadly-based guidance should be prepared, and issued centrally, on the roles and training needs of staff (including court officials and members of the legal profession) involved in court diversionary work.

11.210. The Department of Health and the Home Office should consider, initially with the relevant professional bodies, the scope for formal training for staff involved in court diversion schemes. Such training should reflect the fact that schemes are part of a much broader services network and that they are a means to an end, not an end in themselves.

Care programmes (ST 5.30-5.35)

11.211. Health, social services and criminal justice agencies should agree a joint approach to the staffing, training and financial aspects of operating care programmes for mentally disordered offenders, including for discharged prisoners with continuing mental health care needs. The Department of Health, in conjunction with the Home Office, should also consider the resource implications of what, in practice, would be an extension of the care programme arrangements and should consider issuing guidance to health, social services and criminal justice agencies on the application of care programmes to mentally disordered offenders. *See also 11.16.*

11.212. Contracts to provide mental health care services to prisons should recognise explicitly the need to operate the care programme approach.

11.213. Care programmes should be automatic for patients remitted to prison after mental health treatment in hospital.

Risk assessment (ST 5.36-40)

11.214. Wherever possible, assessments of risk should be undertaken on a multi-disciplinary basis and follow-up should usually form part of a care programme. This issue should be covered in revised guidance on care programmes.

11.215. Agencies should develop and observe clear guidelines for risk assessment and staff should be trained accordingly.

11.216. All staff working with mentally disordered offenders and similar patients should be made aware of relevant guidance on the identification and handling of potentially dangerous or suicidal patients and of procedures for dealing with violence or threats to staff. Wherever necessary, this should be backed-up by practical training.

Central referral points

11.217. Agencies planning to establish a central referral point for the entry of mentally disordered offenders to the health and social services should appraise carefully the need for such a facility and its likely remit. This should take account of staffing and training and other resource considerations, as well as existing referral arrangements and the pre-eminent need to ensure that placements are found speedily. A central point need not be the sole point of referral, especially if an effective central register is maintained (5.43). *Cf 11.22.*

Transport

11.218. The Steering Committee should consider the responsibilites of agencies to provide or fund suitable transport and escorts for mentally disordered offenders (5.47). *See 11.273.*

Report of the academic development advisory group

11.219. There should be a multi-disciplinary framework for developing academic posts, drawing on all relevant parts of health, social and criminal justice services (AD 3.5).

11.220. There should be a clear policy of encouraging the development of multi-disciplinary academic departments with a proper infrastructure (3.5).

11.221. Future academic expansion should take account of the need for a wider national spread (3.6).

11.222. The Department of Health and the Home Office, in consulting professional, academic and other relevant bodies, should give further thought to criteria for determining where future academic expansion should take place (3.7).

11.223. The Department of Health and the Home Office should consider how to achieve academic posts which cover both forensic psychiatry and child and adolescent psychiatry or learning disabilities. Such posts should be part of full academic departments (3.8). *See also 11.131.*

11.224. Early consideration should be given to the establishment of an academic department in the health care of prisoners (3.14).

11.225. The expansion of forensic psychiatry and related staffing proposed by the staffing and training advisory group should be accompanied by a proportionate growth in academic posts (3.16).

11.226. The Department of Health, the Home Office and the Royal College of Psychiatrists should encourage academic links with the private sector (3.17).

11.227. Regional forensic advisers *[or the equivalent]* should have a key role in helping to develop a national strategy for academic development and to begin to identify where new posts could be sited (4.3).

11.228. The Special Hospitals Service Authority should continue to develop academic links and an academic base in a diversity of centres (4.4).

11.229. The academic base for forensic nursing should be expanded within a structured, multi-disciplinary framework (4.6).

11.230. The Department of Health should consider how best to expand the academic base for forensic social work in a multi-disciplinary setting (4.9).

11.231. The Department of Health should consider the creation of academic development centres which can offer research training for social workers on a Regional or supra-Regional basis (4.9).

11.232. The implications for clinical psychology and psychotherapy of expanding the broader academic base should be examined (4.11).

11.233. The Department of Health and the Home Office should discuss with the Department for Education how the policy recommendations of the academic development advisory group might best be funded (5.9). *See FR 7.6.*

Report of the research advisory group

11.234. There should be a more extensive academic base in forensic psychiatry and allied disciplines (RS 2.7).

11.235. A national strategic plan for research in the field of mentally disordered offenders should be developed (2.8).

11.236. A national committee for research on mentally disordered offenders should be established at an early date (2.10).

11.237. The strategic plan for research *(see 11.235)* should be developed according to the principles at RS 3.9 (3.10). *Principles include well-defined goals, flexibility, a multi-disciplinary approach, effective monitoring and coordination of individual projects, and close links between UK and overseas sponsors of research.*

11.238. A network of core departments should be set up, integrating both clinical and research services with a reasonable geographical spread (4.4).

11.239. Each core department should develop its own interests and expertise within the framework of the strategic plan, but there should be close liaison between departments (4.5).

11.240. Each department's primary base should be within a relevant academic institution but each researcher should have a practice element to his or her contract (4.6).

11.241. Each research unit should develop strong links with existing services for mentally disordered offenders, including Special Hospitals, medium secure units and prisons, as well as community services (4.7).

11.242. Increased efforts should be made to disseminate existing reviews, courses and databases and a market survey might be conducted, particularly among the less academic, more practically orientated disciplines, of the best means of ensuring that existing information reaches all appropriate targets. In this context any real gaps in information available should be identified and filled (5.4).

11.243. The research topics at RS 6.8 should be given the highest priority for action within the ambit of the strategic plan (6.9). *See FR 7.10: priorities are starred in figure 9.*

11.244. A standard classification of data for mentally disordered offenders should be set up (7.2).

Report of the finance advisory group

11.245. Planning decisions about services for mentally disordered offenders, at local and national level, should take account of the cost to the agencies which work with this group. This includes the future cost of deterioration in a person's condition when effective early intervention is denied (FN 2.5).

11.246. We welcome the work being undertaken to ensure that social deprivation is adequately reflected in the financial allocations to local health and social services. This should take account of any factors which are identified as being specifically associated with the level of mentally disordered offenders in the population (2.10).

11.247. Decisions about the admission of mentally disordered offenders from police stations, courts and prisons to hospital, and about the transfer of patients between different levels of secure hospital provision, should be based solely on clinical needs and public safety. If not already known, the authority responsible for payment should be established as soon as possible after admission (2.14).

11.248. As a pre-condition for district health authority purchasing of high and medium secure services, there must be suitable arrangements at national and at Regional or sub-Regional level to ensure that the services purchased by districts are comprehensive, of a suitable quality and correspond to the broad principles for services which have been recommended by the Steering Committee at FR 3.3 (4.5).

11.249. The Department of Health should give guidance to Regional Health Authorities on the minimum elements of a forensic psychiatric service, including catchment area services such as court and prison assessment and diversion schemes, as well as services for individual patients. It should then be a Regional responsibility to ensure that districts purchase these services (4.6). *See FN, Annex E.*

Hospital services

11.250. District health authorities (in cooperation with family health service authorities) should be required to accept primary responsibility for meeting the health care, including preventive, needs of mentally disordered offenders in common with the rest of their resident populations. We further recommend that this primary responsibility should remain, even where the individual is receiving specialist treatment outside the DHA boundary (5.5).

11.251. As a strategic aim, district health authorities (possibly as part of a consortium) should become responsible for obtaining the full range of specialist services used by mentally disordered offenders among their populations (5.7).

11.252. NHS managers should, in carrying out financial planning for hospital and community health services, work closely with local authorities, general practitioners, relevant voluntary organisations and criminal justice agencies (5.15).

11.253. Central capital and revenue funding should continue to be made available for the expansion of medium secure provision (5.22).

11.254. We welcome the allocation of £18 million capital in 1992/3 for medium secure provision. Adequate resources should be made available in subsequent years in order to ensure the quickest possible achievement of the 1976 target of 1,000 medium secure places nationally (5.26).

11.255. The so-called "Smith" formula for "enhanced" revenue funding should be abandoned as a basis for calculating additional revenue for medium secure provision and additional places should attract a recurrent revenue allocation at a fixed sum (with allowance for inflation) (5.31). *See 11.256 and FR 5.19; 8.7.*

11.256. The Department of Health should adopt a more flexible approach to releasing a Region's share of enhanced revenue *(see above)* to support urgently needed developments, with the proviso that equity between Regions must be maintained (5.33).

11.257. Adequate revenue and capital funding should be made available to meet the need for medium secure provision over and above the "Glancy" target of 1,000 beds (5.36). *See also 11.274.*

11.258. Districts should, as a medium term aim, become responsible for obtaining high security hospital provision for their residents, but this should be within a framework that ensures the continued availability of an adequate number of high security places nationally (5.39).

11.259. Information about Special Hospital costs attributable to their residents should be made available to all DHAs as soon as possible (5.41).

11.260. Where district health authorities obtain secure hospital provision from the independent sector, they should ensure that other catchment area services are also provided (5.43). *See also 11.272.*

11.261. Arrangements should be made at national level to protect providers with a supra-Regional catchment. Regions should make similar provision for assistance to services with a Regional or sub-Regional catchment (5.46). *See FR 8.7 (iii).*

11.262. NHS hospitals should, wherever it would avoid clinically unacceptable delay in admission of mentally disordered offenders, use the procedures for emergency extra-contractual referrals. The Department of Health should ensure that the provider is paid by the appropriate health authority (5.52).

Community services

11.263. The existing mental illness specific grant should be increased to support expansion of the following services:

> social work involvement in mental health assessment and diversion schemes in courts and prisons;
> social work support in secure psychiatric hospitals;
> care programmes for released mentally disordered prisoners and for those returning to prison from hospital;
> social work involvement in and travel to case conferences at special hospitals, medium secure units and independent sector secure hospitals;
> social work involvement in staffing 24 hour crisis intervention teams; and
> residential and day care services (6.14). *See below.*

11.264. Specific grant provision for mentally disordered offenders should receive 100 per cent central Government funding linked to a five-year spending and development programme, with planning phasing out thereafter (6.18).

11.265. Supplementary credit approvals should be increased to allow capital development of services for mentally disordered offenders. The repayments should be eligible for specific grant (6.20).

11.266. The additional training needs of social services staff involved with services for mentally disordered offenders should be reflected by an increase in the Training Support Programme (6.21). *See also 11.195.*

11.267. An annual sum should be made available for grants to voluntary organisations to contribute to local schemes which would make provision supervised by health and social services for mentally disordered offenders remanded from courts, discharged from hospital or released from prison (6.28).

11.268. The accommodation needs of mentally disordered offenders should be raised by the Department of Health with the Department of the Environment and the Housing Corporation. Community care plans and funding should take account of the related needs for care and support (6.31).

11.269. Statutory and voluntary agencies should consider the scope for the joint purchasing of services for mentally disordered offenders (6.41).

Performance measurement

11.270. The finance advisory group endorsed *(FN 4.8)* the recommendations of the ***performance management group (FN, Annex F)*** that:

    i. as well as individual agencies considering their own measures, a local multi-agency group needs to monitor performance collectively at points in the system which reflect multi-agency activity;

    ii. one or more pilot schemes in particular parts of the country should be established to develop, refine and add to the performance indicators for services for mentally disordered offenders at *figure 10 (see FR 8.17);*

    iii. further work should be carried out to develop methods for carrying out spot audits in hospital, in the criminal justice system and in the community;

    iv. care programme arrangements should be monitored locally, with particular regard in this context to mentally disordered offenders who are discharged from hospital;

    v. the multi-axial assessment system being developed for general psychiatry should be expanded to include mentally disordered offenders;

    vi. consideration should be given to central collection of statistics and to future work in the area of performance measurement.

Final summary report

Victims

11.271. Services dealing with mentally disordered offenders should take account of the needs of victims and offer assistance and staff training where necessary (FR 4.19).

Care programmes and non-statutory services

11.272. The care programme principles in Health Circular (90)23/Local Authority Circular (90)11 should be applied explicitly to mentally disordered offenders being cared for and treated by non-statutory services. It should be the duty of purchasers to stipulate this in contracts (4.23).

Transport

11.273. The Department of Health and the Home Office, in conjunction with other agencies, should examine the need for common guidance on the operation of transport for mentally disordered offenders and other areas of difficulty, such as the suitability of particular forms of transport and arrangements for funding the movement of patients between agencies (5.7).

Medium secure services

11.274. The Department of Health should establish new Regional targets for medium secure provision to reflect assessed need in each Region. These should identify requirements for learning disability and other "special needs" provision and should be kept under review in the light of future needs assessment. Collectively, Regional assessments suggest that at least 1,500 medium secure places will be needed nationally (5.25). *See also 11.59 and 11.127.*

Financing of community care

11.275. The Department of Health and other Government Departments with a direct interest in the accommodation for mentally disordered offenders in the community should take early co-ordinated action to ensure that access to such accommodation is not jeopardised by forthcoming changes in financing of community care (8.13).

The law

11.276. The Department of Health, the Home Office and other interested bodies should consider the suggestions at FR 9.6 for changes to the law, including any consequential effects that these might have on other parts of the present legislation. Any changes should move in tandem with service developments (9.7).

REVIEW OF SERVICES FOR MENTALLY DISORDERED OFFENDERS

MEMBERSHIP OF THE STEERING COMMITTEE

Dr J L Reed *(Chairman)*	Senior Principal Medical Officer, Department of Health.
R J Baxter *(Joint Secretary)*	Grade 5, C3 Division, Home Office.
Professor R S Bluglass	Professor of Forensic Psychiatry, University of Birmingham.
Miss E A Crowther	Director of Social Services, City of London.
A J Davies	Director of Operations, Special Hospitals Service Authority.
A H Fender	General Manager (Purchasing), Salisbury Health Authority.
Professor J Gunn	Department of Forensic Psychiatry, Institute of Psychiatry.
P R Herring	Director of Finance, St Helens and Knowsley Hospital Trust.
I Jewesbury *(Joint Secretary)*	Grade 5, Priority and Health Services Division, Department of Health.
L R Joyce	Chief Executive, Newcastle Mental Health NHS Trust.
Dr J O'Grady	Consultant Psychiatrist, Newcastle General Hospital.
T M O'Sullivan	Governor, HM Prison, Holloway.
E Packer	Clerk to Wimbledon Magistrates.
J Parry	Senior Nurse Manager, Scott Clinic, Rainhill Hospital.
G W Smith CBE	HM Chief Inspector of Probation (lately Chief Probation Officer, Inner London).
J G Smith	Assistant Chief Inspector, Social Services Inspectorate.
Chief Superintendent P Stevens*	Community Involvement and Crime Prevention Branch, Metropolitan Police.
J Tait OBE	Deputy Chief Nursing Officer, Department of Health.
Dr Pamela J Taylor	Head of Medical Services, Special Hospitals Service Authority.
Dr Rosemary Wool	Director, Prison Medical Service.

*Succeeded Commander Sally Hubbard (also of the Metropolitan Police) in June 1991.

To: Regional General Managers
District General Managers
SHA General Managers,
Copy: FHSA General Managers
NHS Trust Chief Executives
Directors of Social Services

NHS *Management Executive*

EL(92)6
5 February 1992

Department of Health
Richmond House
79 Whitehall
London SW1A 2NS
Telephone 071-210 300

Dear Colleague,

Services for mentally disordered offenders and patients with similar needs

1. Ministers have announced that EL(90)190 is being extended to 31 March 1993. This is to ensure a stable base from which to develop services for mentally disordered offenders and patients with similar needs following the current DH/Home Office review.†

2. As a minimum, services for which you are responsible must be able to respond to patient needs at least as effectively as before 1 April 1991. This includes services for patients with "special needs" such as mentally disordered adolescents and those with learning disabilities or personality disorders. Will RGMs please make sure in particular that regional secure units and associated services are maintained at least at their 1990-91 levels. They should also ensure that DHA contracts for mental health services include provision to admit special hospital patients who no longer need maximum security to local facilities as soon as possible.

3. The review Steering Committee's initial reports emphasise the importance of joint working between the NHS, local authorities and other agencies to assess mentally disordered offenders and divert those who need specialised care from police stations, courts and prisons. This is already established policy and advice about it was given in EL(90)168, covering Home Office Circular 66/90. Will all health authorities please ensure that they have adequate liaison arrangements in this field and that the necessary facilities are available locally for patients admitted in this way. RHAs need to make sure that there is adequate cover for the region as a whole, given the range of agencies involved and the sometimes complex relationship between their boundaries.

4. In the light of the Steering Committee's reports Ministers have now announced a large increase in the capital allocation for regional secure units in 1992-93. (see Press notice H92/38 of 27 January 1992). The longer term arrangements for funding services for mentally disordered offenders in the wider context of the new NHS management and financial structures are being considered by a finance advisory group formed as part of the review. This includes the funding of services with a supra-regional catchment.

5. The text of EL(90)190 is enclosed at Annex A; a copy of the Parliamentary written answer is at Annex B. Enquiries about this letter should be addressed to Ms C A Miller, Area 113 Wellington House, 133-155 Waterloo Road, London SE1 8UG, Tel. 071-972 4507.

Yours sincerely,

Andrew Foster

Andrew Foster
Deputy Chief Executive
This letter will be cancelled on 31 March 1993.

---

†Review of Health and Social Services for Mentally Disordered Offenders: overview and reports from advisory groups circulated to RGMs, DGMs and others in November 1991 under cover of a letter from Mr I Jewesbury.

Text of EL(90)190 issued on 28 September 1990

Services for mentally disordered offenders and difficult to manage patients

1.   Minsters have already made it clear that they expect existing services and patient flows to be safeguarded in the move in to the new service from 1 April 1991. Representations have been received from the Home Office, and from legal and other interests, about the need to pay especial attention to those services provided for metally disordered offenders and difficult to manage patients. It is important that these services, and in particular the Regional Secure Units (RSUs) and associated forensic psychiatric services, maintain the capacity to respond at least as effectively post April 1991 as during the preceding period to the needs of those mentally disordered offenders/patients who require NHS in patient treatment.

2.   Apart from provision in the Special Hospitals (1,750 places) the NHS provides about 650 places in RSUs and a further number of places offering lesser security in locally based facilities as well as the normal range of district psychiatric services. A significant proportion of patients in RSUs are admitted following a Court Order, under the Mental Health Act or on transfer from prison or a Special Hospital or on the authority of the Home Secretary. Most of these are treated in facilities outside their district of residence. Predicting demand is therefore difficult, and requires Regional oversight of purchaser intentions to ensure that services will continue to be available as needed.

3.   A number of Regions are continuing regional funding arrangements for RSUs and associated services. Where they are not, RGMs will need to ensure that the contractual arrangements and extra contractual provisions made by DHAs will enable provider units to maintain services at least at the current levels so that their capacity to meet referrals from the prisons, courts and special hospitals and the needs of other difficult to manage patients is fully sustained. All purchasing DHAs should have arrangement to cover patients requiring conditions of medium security for reasons of public safety.

4.   Enquiries about this letter should be addressed to Mr R Freeman, Priority Health Services Division, Room B919, Alexander Fleming House, Elephant and Castle, London SE1 6BY.

DH/Home Office review: Mentally disordered offenders

135 Mr James Paice (C. South East Cambridgeshire):

To ask the Secretary of State for Health, if he will make a statement on the joint Department of Health and Home Office review of health and social services for mentally disordered offenders.

Mr Dorrell

I announce the establishment of the joint review in my reply on 19th December 1990 to my hon. Friend the Member for Bury North, at c.244-5. A Steering Committee was appointed under the chairmanship of Dr. John Reed (Senior Principal Medical Officer, Department of Health). It met first on 31st January 1991 and I am pleased to report that it has made substantial progress.

We are today publishing four consultation documents submitted by the Steering Committee. Copies are available in the Library. These are the reports of three advisory groups that have been examining services provided in the community, in hospital and in prisons, and an overview by the Steering Group itself. We are issuing them to a wide range of interested bodies with the invitation to comment by 31st January 1992.

Between them, the advisory groups have made 87 recommendations aimed at improving the delivery and coordination of care and treatment for mentally disordered offenders. They provide advice on the level and range of health and social services provision that may be needed, as well as the mechanisms required to identify and assess the needs of those who should be diverted from the criminal justice system to more suitable settings. A number of recommendations for the mental health care of prisoners are consistent with the proposals in the White Paper on the prison service, *Custody, Care and Justice* (Cm 1647), and the current consultation paper on contracting for prison health services.

The Steering Committee has set up three further advisory groups which are now beginning work. These are concerned with finance, staffing and training, and research issues. They are due to report in the spring of next year. Work is also being undertaken on performance measurement and quality control, and services for patients with special needs.

The present reports reinforce the Government's policy that mentally disordered offenders who need care and treatment should receive it from the health and personal social services rather than being dealt with in the criminal justice system. They propose also a set of guiding principles for future service provision which we endorse. These are that patients should be cared for:

> with regard to the quality of care and proper attention to the needs of individuals;
>
> as far as possible, in the community, rather than in institutional settings;
>
> under conditions of no greater security than is justified by the degree of danger they present to themselves or others;
>
> in such a way as to maximise their rehabilitation and chances of sustaining an independent life;
>
> as near as possible to their own homes or families, if they have them.

I have already indicated that we do not want necessary action to be delayed merely because the review is in progress. We are considering the present recommendations to identify those which could be implemented at an early date. The Steering Committee have proposed an initial action plan whose main elements are:

> the improvement of inter-agency arrangements for joint working at both planning and operational level;
>
> local assessments of service need, including assessments in each NHS Region before the end of the review of needs for local and medium secure hospital provision;
>
> the continued protection of existing NHS services for mentally disordered offenders, including those for people with certain special needs, pending consideration by the review of arrangements for purchasing services;
>
> to build on the positive response of agencies in the health, social and criminal justices to Home Office Circular 66/90 and to the review itself, and to review good practice guidance in the light of the advisory group reports.

We endorse the direction set by these proposals and will be taking action to follow them up so far as it lies within our direct responsibility. Final decisions will need to take account of the further work initiated by the Steering Committee and of responses to the present consultation exercise.

My right hon. and hon. Friends and I are committed to maintaining the close co-operation which has developed between our Departments through the review. We are very grateful to Dr Reed and his colleagues, and others who have contributed to the advisory groups, for their work so far.

Existing NHS services for mentally disordered offenders are subject to NHS Management Executive Letter (90)190 which directs health authorities to maintain at least the present level of service until December 1991. This guidance is being extended until March 1993 in order to ensure that future planning of these services takes place against a reasonably stable background.

PARLIAMENTARY STATEMENT: 2 JUNE 1992

In a written answer on 2 June 1992 to a Parliamentary Question from Peter Thurnham, MP for Bolton North East, Mr Tim Yeo, Parliamentary Secretary for Community Care, said:

> The review continues to make good progress and is on schedule to complete its work in July.
>
> In his reply on 13th November 1991 to my hon. Friend the Member for South East Cambridgeshire, my hon. Friend the then Parliamentary Under Secretary of State announced that were publishing four initial reports for consultation *[see Annex B]*.
>
> We have received some 200 responses. They have overwhelmingly supported the direction of development proposed in the reports. They also contained many detailed comments, for which we are most grateful.
>
> We are today publishing for consultation five further reports submitted by the Steering Committee chaired by Dr John Reed. Copies are available in the Library. These cover finance, staffing and training, research, academic development, and services for mentally disordered offenders with special needs.
>
> The reports are being issued, as before, to a wide range of interested bodies inviting their comments. Further work in the review is being directed particularly to issues of race and culture, the needs of learning disabled and homeless people, and the role of—and support for—families. These will be reflected in the Steering Committee's final report.
>
> The Government will be considering the recommendations arising from this review as a whole in the light of the final report and the responses to consultation on the present and earlier proposals.
>
> We have already announced increased capital funding for medium secure psychiatric provision of £18 million in the current year, against £3 million in 1991-92.
>
> My right hon. and learned and hon. Friends and I remain committed to close co-operation between our Departments in this field. We are again most grateful to Dr Reed and his colleagues for the work they have done.

HOME OFFICE
Queen Anne's Gate, London SW1H 9AT
Direct line: 01-213
Switchboard: 01-213 3000

Our reference: MNP/90 1/55/8
Your reference:

Tel. No. 0712-273 3000
Fax No. 071-273 2937
Date: 3 September 1990

To Judges of the Crown Court; The Circuit Administrator; The Courts Administrator; The Chief Clerk to the Crown Court; The Clerk to the Justices (with a copy for the information of the Chairman of the Bench); The Chief Officer of Police; The Chief Probation Officer; The Medical Officer, HM Prison; The Clerk to the Magistrates' Courts Committee

cc Director of Public Prosecutions; Clerk to the County County Council; Clerk to the Police Authority; Chairman, Regional Health Authority; Chairman, District Health Authority; The Director of Social Services; The General Manager, Regional Health Authority; The General Manager, District Health Authority

Dear Sir/Madam

Home Office Circular No 66/90

PROVISION FOR MENTALLY DISORDERED OFFENDERS

The purpose of this circular is to draw the attention of the courts and those services responsible for dealing with mentally disordered persons who commit, or are suspected of committing, criminal offences to

    (a) the legal powers which exist; and

    (b) the desirability of ensuring effective co-operation between agencies to ensure that the best use is made of resources and that mentally disordered persons are not prosecuted where this is not required by the public interest.

BACKGROUND

2. It is government policy that, wherever possible, mentally disordered persons should receive care and treatment from the health and social services. Where there is sufficient evidence, in accordance with the principles of the Code for Crown Prosecutors, to show that a mentally disordered person has committed an offence, careful consideration should be given to whether prosecution is required by the public interest. It is desirable that alternatives to prosecution, such as cautioning by the police, and/or admission to hospital, if the person's mental condition requires hospital treatment, or support in the community, should be considered first before deciding that prosecution is necessary. The government recognises that this policy can be effective only if the courts and criminal justice agencies have access to health and social services. This requires consultation and co-operation, and this circular aims to provide guidance on the establishment of a satisfactory working relationship between courts, criminal justice agencies and health and social services.

3. Provisions for mentally disordered offenders in the prison system in England and Wales were studied by an interdepartmental working group of Home Office and DHSS officials which reported in 1987. It recommended that the courts should be encouraged to use the existing provisions of the Mental Health Act, wherever practicable, to enable appropriate mentally disordered persons to be taken into the health system rather than the penal system, and that information should be made available to the courts about the provision of places in special hospitals, regional secure units and local hospitals.

4.   The first point of contact between the criminal justice system and a mentally disordered person is often the police, who may be called to intervene in incidents involving a mentally disordered person. There are a range of powers which are available to the police, and it is important that they establish close working relationships with local health, probation, and social services to assist them in exercising their powers:

(i)   section 136 of the Mental Health Act 1983 provides a constable with a power to remove to a place of safety a person found in a place to which the public have access and who appears to be suffering from mental disorder within the meaning of the Act and in immediate need of care or control if the constable thinks it is necessary to do so in the interests of that person or for the protection of others. The person may be detained for a maximum of 72 hours. The power in this section may be used in relation to persons who have not committed an offence, and to those who have (or are suspected of having) committed an offence, but where it is not considered necessary in the public interest to arrest that person for the offence. Agreement should be reached with local hospitals and local social services departments so that persons detained under section 136 are assessed by a psychiatrist and interviewed by an Approved Social Worker as soon as possible for the purpose of making any necessary arrangements for the person's treatment or care. It is desirable that, wherever possible, the place of safety in which the person might be detained should be a hospital and not a police station. Guidance on the use of section 136 is contained in Chapter 10 of the Department of Health Code of Practice on the implementation of the Mental Health Act 1983 (a copy is attached at Annex A);

(ii)   Section 135 of the 1983 Act empowers a justice of the peace—on information on oath laid by an Approved Social Worker—to issue a warrant authorising any constable to enter specified premises to remove to a place of safety—which should normally be a hospital—a person believed to be suffering from mental disorder who has been, or is being, ill-treated, neglected or not kept under proper control, or who is living alone and unable to care for himself. The warrant will authorise the person's detention in a place of safety for a maximum of 72 hours. The initiative in seeking a warrant will normally rest with an Approved Social Worker. The warrant may apply to any premises within the justice's jurisdiction, including private property to which the police powers under section 136 do not extend;

(iii)   where it is suspected that a mentally disordered person may have committed an offence, consideration should be given— in consultation with the Crown Prosecution Service, where appropriate—to whether any formal action by the police is necessary, particularly where it appears that prosecution is not required in the public interest in view of the nature of the offence. If the suspect is able to meet the requirements for a caution to be administered, he might be cautioned. If the criteria for a caution are not met, the police should consider whether any action need be taken against the suspect. In some cases the public interest might be met by diverting mentally disordered persons from the criminal justice system and finding alternatives to prosecution, such as admission to hospital under sections 2 or 3 or to guardianship under section 7 of the 1983 Act or informal support in the community by social services departments. The development of effective liaison with health and social services authorities will play an essential role in developing satisfactory arrangements to respond constructively in such cases;

(iv)   the questioning of mentally disordered persons suspected of committing offences is subject to the Code of Practice for the Detention, Treatment and Questioning of Persons by Police Officers issued under section 66 of the Police and Criminal Evidence Act 1984. (Annex E of the Code summarises the provisions relating to mentally ill and mentally handicapped persons). Paragraph 9.2 requires the custody officer immediately to call a police surgeon if a person brought to a police station or already detained there appears to be suffering from a mental disorder. In urgent cases the person must be sent to hospital. These requirements apply even if the person makes no request for medical attention. In the case of mentally disordered persons, chief officers of police may find it helpful to arrange with their local health authorities for psychiatrists to fill the role of police surgeon. Chief officers will be aware that even with the protection afforded by the Police and Criminal Evidence Act 1984, some mentally disordered suspects may make confessions which are untrue, and therefore it is always advisable to seek other evidence which may support or reject the suspect's story;

(v) where it is decided that the public interest requires the prosecution of a mentally disordered person for an offence it should be borne in mind that he has the same right as other suspects to bail after charge. If his mental state or other factors, such as homelessness, give rise to difficulties in releasing him on bail, arrangements should be made with the health, probation, and social services to ensure that appropriate support can be provided, such as admission to hospital, where his mental condition warrants it, or to a hostel, if the managers agree. Police bail cannot, of course, be subject to conditions of residence or medical treatment, but satisfactory arrangements to provide for these on a voluntary basis may enable the police to release the suspect on bail rather than to detain him pending his appearance before the magistrates' court;

(vi) after a mentally disordered person has been charged, wherever possible arrangements should be made with the health, probation, and social services for his assessement with a view to ensuring that he receives any medical treatment that may be necessary, and that the Crown Prosecution Service and court can be advised of any particular bail conditions or, after conviction, disposal that may be appropriate to his circumstances. At Annex B to this circular is a note outlining court psychiatric assessment arrangements which have been established at certain central London and at Peterborough magistrates' courts to secure expert medical advice when required. Chief officers of police may wish to explore with their local chief probation officers and health authorities the possibility of setting up similar arrangements to ensure that suspects who are thought to be mentally disordered and in need of medical assessment should be seen by a psychiatrist as soon as possible.

5. A small minority of cases involving mentally disordered persons result in findings by the Crown Court of unfitness to plead under the provisions of the Criminal Procedure (Insanity) Act 1964. Details of the consequences of such a finding are set out in paragraph 13 below. It is important to note, however, that although the accused is admitted to hospital as if subject to a hospital order and a restriction order without limit of time, a finding of unfitness to plead is not a disposal by the court. The intention of the Act is that the accused should return to court to stand trial, wherever possible, if his condition improves sufficiently to enable him to do so. It is, therefore, essential that, where a person is found unfit to plead, all the relevant evidence should be preserved either until the accused is remitted for trial, or until formal notification is received from the Crown Prosecution Service or Home Office that a trial will not be held.

CROWN PROSECUTION SERVICE

6. Where proceedings are instituted against a person by the police, the papers will be referred to the Crown Prosecution Service which will review the sufficiency of the evidence and consider carefully whether or not the public interest requires a prosecution in accordance with the Code for Crown Prosecutors. Any information provided by the police with the papers regarding that person's mental condition, or discussions held with other agencies to consider the advisability of diverting him from court, will be taken into account. It will be important to distinguish between those forms of mental disorder which are made worse by the institution of criminal proceedings and those forms of mental disorder which come about by reason of the institution of criminal proceedings. Where the Service is satisfied that the probable effect upon a person's mental health outweighs the interests of justice in the particular case, it will consider discontinuing the proceedings. Where the form of mental disorder is present without there being any indication that proceedings will have an adverse effect, the Crown Prosecutor will take account of the public interest in attempting to ensure that the offence will not be repeated as well as having regard to the welfare of the person in question.

MAGISTRATES' COURTS

7. Mentally disordered persons have the same rights as other persons, including a right to bail. A mentally disordered person should never be remanded to prison simply to receive medical treatment or assessment. It is desirable for the court to receive professional advice at as early a stage as possible on facilities which may be available to assist it with mentally disordered persons. Annex B to this circular describes court psychiatric assessment arrangements at certain central London and at Peterborough magistrates' courts. These enable the courts to receive speedy medical advice and to ensure that, where appropriate, arrangements can be made quickly to admit a mentally disordered person to hospital, for example as a condition of bail or, with the agreement of the hospital managers, under section 35 of the Mental Health Act 1983 following conviction.

Where neither of these courses is applicable but the accused person nevertheless requires admission to hospital for assessment or treatment, the health and social services can be asked to consider using their civil powers of admission under sections 2 or 3 of the Act.

8.   In considering cases involving mentally disordered persons magistrates may wish to bear in mind the possible courses of action which may be open to them. These include:

(i)   where the Crown Prosecution Service decides to proceed with a case, the court will be required to consider the question of bail in the normal way. In cases where medical treatment is considered desirable this may be achieved as a condition of bail, such as requiring residence at a hospital of attendance at an outpatient clinic, although the bailed person cannot be compelled to comply with treatment under these circumstances. Magistrates will wish also to bear in mind the desirability of arranging for a medical report on the accused's condition to be prepared on bail. Their attention is drawn to Annex C of this circular, which describes the multi-agency assessment scheme operating in Hertfordshire;

(ii)   in cases where an accused person has been convicted of an offence punishable with imprisonment, or has been charged with such an offence and the court is satisfied he did the act or made the omission charged, and it is considered necessary to remand him in custody rather than on bail, the attention of magistrates is drawn to the power of the court under section 35 of the 1983 Act to remand to hospital provided it is satisfied in accordance with section 35(4) that arrangements have been made for the admission of the accused within a period of seven days. This power should be used wherever possible to obtain a medical report on an accused person's condition, providing the court has written or oral evidence from a doctor who is approved under section 12(2) of the Act as having special experience in the diagnosis and treatment of mental disorder, that there is reason to suspect that the accused is suffering from mental illness, psychopathic disorder, mental impairment or severe mental impairment and the court is of the opinion that it would be impracticable for a report on the accused's mental condition to be made if he were remanded on bail. Normally the local psychiatric hospital or unit in a general hospital will be able to provide adequate arrangements for the assessment of mentally disordered persons, but in addition most regional health authorities are able to provide secure hospital accommodation in cases where this is necessary, and places may be sought in a special hospital in respect of persons who are thought to require treatment in conditions of special security because of their violent, dangerous, or criminal propensities. At Annex D is a note of health service hospital facilities. Magistrates' courts are requested to consider with their Regional Health Authority the establishment of working arrangements to ensure that appropriate hospital facilities can be made available speedily when necessary;

(iii)   where a person suffering from mental illness or severe mental impairment is charged with an offence punishable on conviction with imprisonment (other than where the sentence is fixed by law), a magistrates' court has power under section 37(3) of the 1983 Act to make a hospital order without convicting him provided the court is satisfied that the accused did the act or made the omission charged, and that on the evidence of two registered medical practitioners, one of whom is approved under section 12(2) of the Act, the accused is suffering from mental disorder of a nature or degree which makes it appropriate for him to be detained in hospital for treatment. In the case of psychopathic disorder or mental impairment the court must also be satisfied, on the same evidence, that such treatment is likely to alleviate or stabilise the condition. Before making an order, the court must be satisfied under section 37(4) that arrangements have been made for the offender's admission to hospital within 28 days of an order being made. The requirements for determining whether the offence should be tried summarily or on indictment need not necessarily be complied with, nor is a trial necessary, before exercising this power. However, its exercise will usually require the consent of those acting for the defendant if he is under a disability so that he cannot be tried (see *R v Lincolnshire (Kesteven) Justices, ex p. O'Connor* [1983] 1AER 901);

(iv)   where a mentally disordered person is convicted of an offence the court will wish to consider whether a non-penal disposal may be appropriately imposed. These include:

(a)   a hospital order under section 37 of the 1983 Act in cases where the accused person is convicted of an offence punishable with imprisonment (other than where the sentence is fixed by law), if the court is satisfied on evidence from two registered medical practitioners, one of whom is approved under section 12(2) of the Act, that the offender is suffering from mental disorder of a nature or degree which makes it appropriate for him to be detained in hospital for treatment, and that in the case of psychopathic disorder or mental impairment the treatment is likely to alleviate or stabilise the condition. The court must also be satisfied that, in accordance with section 37(4), arrangements have been made for the offender's admission to hospital within twenty eight days;

(b) an interim hospital order under section 38 of the 1983 Act. To assist the court and hospital in determining whether it is appropriate to make a hospital order in respect of an offender, the courts may make an interim hospital order so that the offender's response in hospital can be evaluated without any irrevocable commitment on either side to this method of dealing with the offender if it should prove unsuitable.

Before making an interim hospital order the court must be satisfied on evidence from two doctors, one of whom is approved under section 12(2) of the Act, that the offender is suffering from mental disorder such as makes it reasonable to suppose that a hospital order might be appropriate. It must also be satisfied in accordance with section 38(4) that arrangements have been made for the offender's admission to hospital within 28 days;

(c) a guardianship order under section 37 of the 1983 Act in cases where the offender is convicted of an offence punishable with imprisonment (other than where the sentence is fixed by law), placing the offender under the guardianship of the local social services authority or a person approved by it, provided he has reached the age of 16 and the court is satisfied on evidence from two registered medical practitioners, one of whom is approved under section 12(2) of the Act, that the mental disorder is of a nature or degree which warrants reception into guardianship. By virtue of section 37(6) a guardianship order is not to be made unless the court is satisfied that the authority or person in question is willing to receive the offender.

The purpose of guardianship is primarily to ensure that the offender receives care and protection rather than medical treatment, although the guardian does have powers to require the offender to attend for medical treatment. The effect of a guardianship order is to give the guardian power to require the offender to live at a specific place (this may be used to discourage the offender from sleeping rough or living with people who may exploit or mistreat him, or ensure that he resides at a particular hostel), to attend specific places at specified times for medical treatment, occupation, education, or training, and to require access to the offender to be given at the place where the offender is living to any doctor, approved social worker, or other person specified by the guardian. This power could be used, for example, to ensure the offender did not neglect himself;

(d) a probation order with a condition of psychiatric treatment under section 3 of the Powers of Criminal Courts Act 1973. This is a normal probation order which has been adapted to meet the needs of an offender who does not need to be detained in a hospital, but who is suffering from a mental condition which can be treated and needs treatment. A probation order may not be made unless the Court is satisfied that arrangements have been made for the treatment which the court intends to specify in the Order, including arrangements for the offender's reception where he is to be required to submit to treatment as an in-patient. The court may make a probation order in the normal way, with the consent of the offender; and if it is satisfied on the evidence of a doctor approved as having special experience in the diagnosis or treatment of mental disorder that the offender needs treatment for his mental condition but does not need to be detained in hosptial, the court may include in the probation order a requirement that he undergoes medical treatment with a view to the improvement of his mental condition. A condition of residence at a hospital can be attached to the probation order, if appropriate, even where formal detention under the Mental Health Act is not indicated. The court may also wish to call for a social inquiry report to assist it in reaching a decision in such cases. The offender may be required to undertake treatment for the whole of the period of the probation order, or for part of it. If he fails to comply with the requirements of the probation order, the offender is in breach of probation and may be dealt with in the same way as any other offender who is in breach of probation;

(e) discharge, either absolute or conditional, so that arrangements may be made on an informal basis for the offender to receive any necessary medical treatment or social work support. Under such a disposal, however, treatment may not be adminstered compulsorily, unless the offender is subsequently detained under the civil powers of the 1983 Act.

9.   It is open to any magistrates' court which is minded to make a hospital or interim hospital order in respect of any person to ask the Regional Health Authority under the provisions of section 39 of the 1983 Act for information about hospitals which can accommodate that person (see paragraph 15 below).

CROWN COURT

10.   In considering cases involving mentally disordered persons the Crown Court may wish to bear in mind its powers to obtain a medical report by:

(i) remanding on bail with a condition of attendance at, or residence in, a hospital for the purpose of medical assessment;

(ii) remanding to hospital under the provisions of section 35 of the 1983 Act an accused person suffering from mental illness, psychopathic disorder, mental impairment or severe mental impairment who is awaiting trial for an offence punishable with imprisonment, or who has been arraigned but not yet sentenced or otherwise dealt with.

This power may be exercised where the court is satisfied on the evidence of a doctor, who is approved under section 12(2) of the Act that there is reason to suspect the accused is suffering from mental disorder, and the court is of the opinion that it would be impracticable for a medical report to be made if he were remanded on bail. The court must also be satisfied in accordance with section 37(4) that the accused will be admitted to hospital within 7 days. (This power may not be exercised in respect of a person convicted before the court if the sentence for the offence of which he has been convicted is fixed by law.)

11.   The Crown Court has power under section 36 of the 1983 Act to remand an accused person (other than a person charged with an offence the sentence for which is fixed by law) to hospital for treatment. The court must be satisfied on the evidence of two registered medical practitioners, one of whom must be approved under section 12(2) of the Act, that the accused is suffering from mental illness or severe mental impairment of a nature or degree which makes it appropriate for him to be detained in hospital for medical treatment. The court must also be satisfied, in accordance with section 36(3), that the accused will be admitted to hospital within 7 days. The court may find this power helpful when considering cases of mentally disordered persons who may be unfit to plead but whose mental condition might improve as a result of medical treatment.

12.   Cases may arise where an accused person, who has been remanded in prison custody, is transferred by the Home Secretary to hospital for urgent treatment under the provisions of section 48 of the 1983 Act. If it appears to the Crown Court in such a case that it is impracticable or inappropriate to bring that person before the court, the court may, in accordance with section 51(5), make a hospital order (with or without a restriction order) in his absence and, in the case of a person awaiting trial, without convicting him. Before doing so the court must be satisfied on the written or oral evidence of at least two registered medical practitioners, one of whom is approved under section 12(2) of the Act, that the accused is suffering from mental illness or severe mental impairment which makes it appropriate for him to be detained in hospital for treatment, and that it is proper to make such an order.

13.   In cases where the accused is found to be unfit to plead under the provisions of section 4 of the Criminal Procedure (Insanity) Act 1964, the court is required by section 5 of the Act to make an order that the accused be admitted to such hospital as may be specified by the Secretary of State. This may be a special hospital, a regional secure unit or a local hospital, depending on the gravity of the alleged offence and the apparent risk to the public. The accused is treated as though subject to a hospital order and a restriction order without limit of time made under the provisions of sections 37 and 41 of the Mental Health Act 1983. In view of the nature of this disposal, courts are asked to bear in mind their power under section 4(2) of the 1964 Act to postpone consideration of the defendant's fitness to plead until anytime up to the opening of the case for the defence. This provides an opportunity to test the prosecution case and may reduce the likelihood of an innocent

person being detained. This may be particularly important in the case of persons who appear to be suffering from severe mental impairment. Their condition is unlikely to change after receiving medical treatment and consequently they may never be able to benefit from a normal trial. Where a person is found unfit to plead the Home Secretary will arrange for his case to be reviewed at six monthly intervals during the first two years of his detention in hospital to consider his fitness to stand trial, and he would normally expect to remit that person for trial should he receive medical advice that he is fit to plead. If, at the end of two years, the Home Secretary is advised that he remains unfit to plead he will review the continuing need for the restriction order under section 42(1) of the 1983 Act and will terminate it if he concludes it is unnecessary for the protection of the public from serious harm.

14. If a mentally disordered person is convicted of an offence the court will wish to consider the suitability of non-penal disposals. These include:

  (i) a hospital order in cases where a person is convicted of an offence (other than one for which the sentence is fixed by law) punishable with imprisonment, if the court is satisfied, in accordance with the provisions of section 37(2) of the 1983 Act, on the evidence of two registered medical practitioners, one of whom is approved under section 12(2) of the Act, that the offender is suffering from mental disorder of a nature or degree which makes it appropriate for him to be detained in hospital for treatment, and that, in the case of psychopathic disorder or mental impairment, the treatment is likely to alleviate or stabilise the condition. The court must also be satisfied that, in accordance with the provisions of section 37(a), arrangements have been made for the offender's admission to hospital within twenty eight days. In addition to the special hospitals (Ashworth (formerly Moss Side and Park Lane Hospitals), Broadmoor and Rampton), which provide treatment in conditions of special security for persons with violent, dangerous, or criminal propensities, most regional health authorities provide a range of hospital facilities for the treatment of mentally disordered offenders, including secure units. At Annex D is a note of health service hospital facilities;

  (ii) an interim hospital order (see paragraph 8.iv.(b) above);

  (iii) a restriction order. In any case where it makes a hospital order under section 37 of the 1983 Act, the court may also make a restriction order under section 41 where it appears necessary for the protection of the public from serious harm. The decision on whether to make the order rests with the court and does not depend upon the agreement of the hospital or the doctor in whose care the patient will be placed, although at least one of the doctors whose evidence is taken into account in making a hospital order must have given oral evidence in court. In reaching its decision the court must take into account the nature of the offence, the antecedents of the offender, and the risk of his committing further offences if set at large. (The law governing the making of restriction orders was clarified by the Court of Appeal in *R v Birch* [1989] CLR June 296.) A restriction order may be either for a specified period or without limit of time, and may be terminated at any time by the Home Secretary under section 42(1). The effect of a restriction order is that the patient may not be discharged (except by a Mental Health Review Tribunal), granted leave of absence, or transferred to another hospital without the consent of the Home Secretary. Restricted patients are generally discharged from hospital subject to conditions of residence and supervision by a doctor and a social worker or probation officer, remaining liable to recall to hospital by the Home Secretary for a period after their discharge. Where circumstances warrant it, however, such patients can be absolutely discharged from hospital instead of having to complete a period of supervised living in the community;

  (iv) a guardianship order (see paragraph 8.iv.(c) above);

  (v) a probation order (see paragraph 8.iv.(d) above);

  (vi) discharge. Where the court is satisfied that, following conviction, the public interest requires no formal sentence or other disposal it is open to the court to discharge the offender, either absolutely or conditionally, particularly if it believes that satisfactory arrangements for the care and treatment of the offender can be made on an informal basis.

In considering these options, the court may find it useful to involve the Crown Court liaison probation officer in approaching the health authorities or social services departments or in making appropriate arrangements for the preparation of a social inquiry report.

15. To assist the courts in deciding whether to make a hospital or interim hospital order, section 39 of the 1983 Act places a duty on Regional Health Authorities to respond to requests from courts for information about hospitals which could provide accomodation for people in respect of whom the courts are considering making hospital orders. This obliges Regional Health Authorities to inform the court as to the facilities they provide for detained patients, including those who may require treatment in appropriate conditions of security; and it will also enable the Regional Health Authority to advise in cases where there is some room for doubt as to the patient's normal place of residence or other factor determining the appropriate hospital within whose catchment area he falls. The intention is to provide a court with all possible assistance short of removing the obligation in section 37(4) of the 1983 Act to be satisfied that the necessary arrangements have been made before making a hospital order, in cases where the necessary criteria for a hospital order are satisfied and it is minded to make one, but no hospital place has been made available. Regional Health Authorities have been encouraged to make standing arrangements for meeting such requests for information from courts, and it is intended that these arrangements will reduce the number of cases in which a hospital order appears suitable but the court is frustrated in the search for a place. In cases where it is desired to make use of this provision, the clerk of the court should contact the Regional Medical Officer or solicitor for the Regional Health Authority covering the area from which the offender appears to come. (There is no longer any scope for disputes between Regional Health Authorities as to responsibility for dealing with the enquiry, as any Authority approached by the court is under a statutory duty to provide information about hospitals "in its region or elsewhere" at which arrangements could be made for the person to be admitted. If the Authority first contacted believes it to be more appropriate for another Authority to respond, it will only be able to pass on responsibility if the second Authority agrees.)

16. Where a court is satisfied that at the time of committing the act with which he is charged the accused was labouring under such a defect of reason from disease of the mind as not to know the nature and quality of the act he was doing or, if he did know it, that he did not know he was doing what was wrong, it shall return the special verdict of not guilty by reason of insanity. In accordance with the provisions of section 5(1) of the Criminal Procedure (Insanity) Act 1964 the court is required to make an order that the accused be admitted to such hospital as may be specified by the Home Secretary (the level of security being determined by the seriousness of the offence and the apparent risk of further offending), where he will be detained as though subject to a hospital order and restriction order without limit of time made under sections 37 and 41 of the Mental Health Act 1983.

PROBATION SERVICE

17. The probation service should act as part of a network of agencies (social services, health services, voluntary organisations) providing accommodation, care and treatment in the community for mentally disordered offenders. Information about facilities for accommodation, treatment, education, supervision etc should be pooled, and there should be a shared list of contact points with telephone numbers for each agency. (In some areas it may be sensible for the probation service to take the lead in co-ordinating this network, but elsewhere the lead might be taken by a voluntary organisation or by the social services with their responsibility for care in the community.) The special role of the probation service is:

— to provide information to the courts for bail and sentencing decisions;
— to provide information to the Crown Prosecution Service in connection with bail information schemes;
— to provide bail and probation hostels and other accommodation projects for offenders and persons on bail;
— to provide for the throughcare and supervision of offenders released from prison on licence and parole.

Chief Probation Officers are asked to establish liaison arrangements with other agencies to ensure that the probation service can carry out these tasks effectively. At Annex E is a note outlining seminars and training courses organised by the West Yorkshire and the Greater Manchester Probation Services and by the Northern Regional Committee for Probation Staff Development which chief officers might find helpful as examples of good practice in encouraging co-operation with other agencies and with the courts.

18. When a mentally disordered person is arrested and charged, the probation service should play its part in diverting him or her from custodial remand. They can do this in several ways. If there is a bail information scheme, the probation officer will visit the accused in police custody to interview him and obtain information which, if verified, can be passed on the Crown Prosecution Service to inform the bail decision. Mentally disordered persons may be particularly at risk of

being remanded in custody, because their circumstances and way of life may be unstable. Good liaison between the bail information scheme, the police, the health service and social services will therefore be particularly important. If in-patient treatment is not warranted, the probation officer may be able to identify suitable accommodation in a bail hostel or lodging scheme organised by the probation service, or by the social services. Intervention at this stage can prevent unnecessary remands to prison establishments.

19.   If there is no bail information scheme the first contact may not occur until the accused's first court appearance. The court will have the range of options described in paragraph 8(i) and (ii) above. In particular, mentally disordered persons may be remanded to hospital by the courts under the provisions of section 35 and 36 of the Mental Health Act 1983. In other cases it is open to the courts to remand the accused on bail with a condition of residence in a hospital or of attendance at a hospital. Persons whose condition is not such as to require in-patient treatment may be considered for placement in a bail hostel where this is desirable to avoid a remand in custody. Or they may be remanded on bail with other conditions (eg living at a specified address). The court duty probation officer can help the court by advising on ways of avoiding a custodial remand making use of resources and treatment available in the community. This will succeed only if the probation service has good liaison with, and support from, other agencies, especially the health service and the local authority social services, whose responsibilities are described at Annex F.

20.   When mentally disordered persons are convicted of offences, the court will wish to consider the possibility of a community disposal. In cases where detention in hospital for treatment under the provisions of section 37 of the 1983 Act is not considered necessary, but the offender's mental condition is still treatable, a probation order with a condition of psychiatric treatment may be given. If the offender's condition is not treatable, a probation order may be made without a condition of treatment, but with other conditions or arrangements which make for effective supervision. These may include residence at a probation hostel or other community care arrangements made by the social services or a voluntary organisation. It is important that the court should have a social inquiry report available to it in addition to medical advice. The SIR should set out the full range of sentencing options which may be suitable, and give details of the type of supervision and accommodation which could and would be provided in the community. There should be liaison between probation officer, author of the medical report and the offender's lawyer about an appropriate recommendation to the court.

21.   It is important that all accused persons who are likely to be suitable candidates for probation orders are identified at as early a stage as possible and that arrangements are made quickly for their medical assessment. Chief Probation Officers are asked to review their procedures, in consultation with police, the courts, social services and health authorities, to ensure that they identify candidates for community disposals at an early stage in the prosecution process and assist in achieving a swift disposal of the case by the courts. (At Annex C is a brief description of a multi-agency assessment scheme in operation in Hertfordshire).

22.   The effectiveness of probation orders with a condition of treatment depends on close co-operation, understanding and communication between the probation service and local psychiatric services, and is aided by the presence at local level of psychiatric staff with an interest in forensic psychiatry. It would be helpful for each probation area to draw up its own code of practice for probation officers undertaking supervision of a mentally disordered offender, defining lines of responsibility and accountability (eg clarifying of boundaries between the responsible medical officer and the probation officer, especially where both are carrying statutory responsibilities).

PRISON MEDICAL SERVICE

23.   Consolidated guidance will be issued shortly to the prison medical service in a circular instruction from the Director of the Prison Medical Service. This reminds medical officers when examining remand prisoners on reception into prison to be alert for signs of mental disorder. Any prisoner who is suffering from mental illness or severe mental impairment of a nature or degree which makes it appropriate for him to be detained in hospital for medical treatment and is in urgent need of hospital treatment, should be recommended for transfer to hospital in accordance with the provisions of section 48 of the Mental Health Act 1983. Medical officers are encouraged to discuss with C3 Division any case where there is doubt about what initiative to take or where there is any difficulty in securing a hospital place. Medical officers should also seek to indentify those remand prisoners who might benefit from medical treatment after conviction, for example

by means of a hospital order, psychiatric probation order, or guardianship order. In such cases they should offer advice to the court and, where appropriate, should seek the assistance of the probation service, for example in arranging for a psychiatric probation or a guardianship order to be made by the court.

24. In the case of sentenced prisoners, medical officers are reminded of the need to arrange the transfer to hospital under section 47 of the Mental Health Act 1983 as soon as possible during the course of their sentences of those prisoners suffering from mental illness, psychopathic disorder, mental impairment, or severe mental impairment of a nature or degree which makes it appropriate for them to be detained in hospital for treatment. Medical officers should ask a consultant psychiatrist from the catchment area hospital or regional secure unit, or special hospital covering the prisoner's home to visit as soon as possible to assess the prisoner and to arrange his admission to their hospital, taking account of the level of security which is required. Recommendations for transfer from two registered medical practitioners, at least one of whom is approved for the purposes of section 12 of the Mental Health Act 1983 as having special experience in the diagnosis or treatment of mental disorder, should then be put forward to C3 Division. Medical officers are encouraged to discuss any cases where there is doubt, or where difficulty is experienced in finding a hospital place, with C3 Division.

CONCLUSION

25. It is the government's policy to divert mentally disordered persons from the criminal justice system in cases where the public interest does not require their prosecution. Where prosecution is necessary it is important to find suitable non-penal disposals wherever appropriate and the police, courts, and probation service are asked to work together with their local health and social services to make effective use of the provisions of the Mental Health Act 1983 and of the services which exist to help the mentally disordered. They are also asked to ensure that all their officers are aware of this circular, and to consider any training which is necessary to equip them in their contracts with mentally disordered persons.

26. In summary:

    (i) Chief Officers of Police are asked to ensure that, taking account of the public interest, consideration is always given to alternatives to prosecuting mentally disordered offenders, including taking no further action where appropriate, and that effective arrangements are established with local health and social services authorities to ensure their speedy involvement when mentally disordered persons are taken into police custody;

    (ii) Courts are asked to ensure that alternatives to custody are considered for all mentally disordered persons, including bail before sentence, and that persons who are in need of medical treatment are not sent to prison. The attention of court clerks is drawn, in particular, to the desirability of establishing arrangements in co-operation with the probation service and the local health and social services authorities, for speedy access to professional advice for the court to assist it in its decision making;

    (iii) Chief Probation Officers are asked to ensure that effective arrangements are established to provide courts with information and advice to enable them to make use of alternatives to imprisonment in dealing with mentally disordered offenders. Attention is drawn to the need to co-operate with local health and social services authorities to provide professional advice to courts and to facilitate a wider use of treatment and non custodial disposals, including remands on bail before sentence and psychiatric probation orders and guardianship orders, where appropriate, after conviction; and

    (iv) Prison medical officers are asked to ensure that action is taken to arrange transfer to hospital under the provisions of section 48 of the Mental Health Act 1983 in respect of any mentally ill or severely mentally impaired person remanded in custody who appears to require urgent treatment in hospital, and to consider advising the courts of the suitability of any other mentally disordered person on remand for treatment as part of a non-custodial disposal, such as a psychiatric probation order or guardianship order, after conviction. Prison medical officers are asked to ensure that action is taken to arrange the transfer to hospital under the provisions of section 47 of the Mental Health Act 1983 of any sentenced prisoner who appears to require treatment in hospital for mental disorder.

27.   Enquiries about this circular should be addressed to Robert Wallich, C3 Division, Home Office, 50 Queen Anne's Gate, London S.W.1 (telephone 071-273-3118).

Yours faithfully

Robert Baxter

Robert Baxter
C3 Division

The annexes to this circular, are omitted. They are reproduced at Annex B of the report of the community advisory group.

REPORT OF THE OFFICIAL WORKING GROUP ON SERVICES FOR PEOPLE WITH SPECIAL NEEDS*

THE DISCUSSION PAPERS: AN OVERVIEW

1.   This annex (adapted from the report of the special needs working group) identifies some key points raised in the discussion papers on services for people with special or differing needs. Recommendations are at paragraphs 11.88-114 of the main report.

People with brain injury [Discussion Paper 1]

2.   Brain injury occurs most commonly in young adult males and among elderly people. Although relatively few people suffer longer-term physical effects, the majority will experience some cognitive problems which could lead to disordered, including, in some cases, offensive or offending, behaviour. This is sometimes compounded by an inability to come to terms with what has happened and an unwillingness to involve clinicians. The police and others in the criminal justice system should be encouraged to recognise the presence of brain injury (although, in practice, this is often indentified specifically only after specialised assessment).

3.   *Paper 1* describes the need for effective early intervention and a coordinated approach to rehabilitation that involves, as necessary, a range of staff and services. Attention to the needs of families, carers and employers, possibly over a long period, must be regarded as part of this process. Access to specialised rehabilitation units is often limited, although the Department of Health is currently funding a number of demonstration schemes and an evaluation study. Offenders with major personality disorders are often difficult to handle unless diagnosed as having a "psychopathic disorder" under section 1(2) of the Mental Health Act 1983.

People who are deaf or hearing impaired [Discussion Paper 2]

4.   Mentally disordered offenders who are deaf or have impaired hearing face a range of communication problems, including the risk that others may not understand them. *Paper 2* describes the services that may need to be available at various points of the system, including effective screening and, for a small number of patients, access to specialised provision, possibly at Regional or supra-Regional level. These aspects need to be addressed in agencies' wider strategies for mentally disordered offenders.

5.   Staff will require training to recognise and respond to hearing problems. Professional interpreters and speech therapists will be needed in some cases. Programmes for profoundly deaf people should include educational opportunities and the chance to mix with other deaf people. The voluntary sector has a major role.

Substance misusers [Discussion Paper 3]

6.   Both alcohol and drug dependence are classified by the World Health Organisation as mental disorders, but they do not in themselves permit detention under the Mental Health Act. 1 in 4 men and 1 in 12 women in England and Wales are estimated to drink above sensible limits, with possible risk of physical, psychological or social harm. Gunn *et al* (1991) found that 8.6 per cent of sentenced adult male prisoners and 12 per cent of female prisoners had a diagnosis of alcohol misuse. The size of the drug misuse problem is difficult to estimate; in 1989, the number of "hard drug" addicts notified to the Home Office was about 15,000. Among sentenced prisoners, as many as 1 in 10 men and 1 in 4 women had a primary diagnosis on arrest of drug dependence or misuse (Gunn).

7.   *Paper 3* describes Government action to tackle the problems, including the need for an active health education programme, advisory and counselling services, detoxification and rehabilitation facilities, and a coordinated approach by all agencies involved, including the voluntary sector, which here too plays an important part. *The Health of the Nation* White Paper (Cm 1986, 1992) proposed targets for reducing alcohol consumption.

---

*To be published by HMSO in a revised edition as *Special Issues and Differing Needs (volume 5 of review reports)*.

8. Mentally disordered offenders are a relatively small group among substance misusers, but they often display a multiplicity of problems calling for a high level of services. There need to be effective links between general mental illness, specialised forensic, and substance misuse services provided in a range of settings. Strategic links with Regional alcohol misuse coordinators and Regional drug abuse committees, as well as criminal justice agencies, are also important. Multi-agency groups for mentally disordered offenders, as proposed by the earlier advisory groups (CR 3.26-3.29), and area committees for the criminal justice system (CR 3.30-3.32) should be well-placed to help effect these.

Sex offenders with mental health care needs [Discussion Paper 4]

9. Policy on services for sex offenders involves a diversity of interests at both national and local level. These require close coordination. Key issues include:

    (i) the introduction by the prison service of structured programmes which attach importance to multi-disciplinary discharge plans;

    (ii) the implications of the Criminal Justice Act 1991 for health and social services providing treatment and supervision in the community and advice at the point of sentence;

    (iii) the role of the Inter-Departmental Group on Child Abuse;

    (iv) current evaluations of treatment programmes; and

    (v) the establishment of a new professional organisation, the National Association for the Development of Work with Sex Offenders.

10. *Paper 4,* which reflects the collective views of a number of interests at national level, and which was also considered by the research advisory group (see below), provides an analysis of the current position. It points the way to further collaborative work.

11. The research advisory group considered the need for research and evaluation of aspects of work with sex offenders, as well as the scope for collating and disseminating the results. It identified four principal areas in which research is required:

    (i) looking more closely at the criminal careers of sex offenders;

    (ii) the cause and continuation of the paraphilias;

    (iii) a reliable classification of offending and disorder;

    (iv) the evaluation of management strategies and treatments of offenders and their victims.

Suicide prevention [Discussion Paper 5]

12. *Paper 5,* highlights growing concern about the incidence of suicide and self-harm among mentally disordered people, especially in prison. It notes that, in 1990, a third of self-inflicted prison deaths were of people with a history of mental illness. The staffing and training advisory group has extended an earlier recommendation of local consultant involvement in Prison Suicide Prevention Management Groups (PR 5.22) by proposing the automatic involvement of a range of health and personal social services staff.

13. Suicide rates are regarded as one useful outcome measure of the effectiveness of mental illness services. A positive approach to performance measurement should help, over time, to minimise suicides but is only part of the picture. There is a particular need for effective identification of people at risk and a coordinated approach to follow-up care. Care programmes have an important role to play. Staff will need guidance on how to approach this difficult and sensitive area. DHSS Health Notice (84) 25/Local Authority Social Services Letter (84)5 provides current guidance on the management of deliberate self-harm, but this may need to be supplemented. *The Health of the Nation* (*op cit*, 1992) has established a target for the reduction of the overall suicide rate by at least 15 per cent by the year 2000 (*i.e.* from 11·1 per 100,000 of the population in 1990 to no more than 9·4) and that of severely mentally ill people by a third is the same period (*ibid*, Section C).

Children and adolescents [Discussion Paper 6]

14. Adolescence is a stage of development rather than a precise age range. For the purpose of the report, 10-20 was taken as the approximate range of the client group. The main considerations are that young people receive the care and treatment they need in surroundings that best meet their interests, that they do not fall between child and adult services, and that the *transition to adulthood* (see Department of Health (1991) *The Children Act 1989 Guidance and Regulations— Volume 6: Children with Disabilities)*, Chapter 16); is properly managed. On rare occasions some children under the age of 10 (*i.e.* below the age of criminal responsibility) will require special

attention. The Health Advisory Service report, *Bridges Over Troubled Waters* (1986), is currently the principal source of general guidance on child and adolescent psychiatric services.

15. There is no accurate estimate of the prevalence of mentally disordered adolescent offenders, although offending among young people aged 14-17 is higher per head of population than that of any other age group and over 10 per cent of the general adolescent population are thought to require some psychiatric intervention. Further research is needed. Of about 170 referrals annually to the one NHS secure unit for mentally disordered adolescents (the Gardener unit near Manchester), 68 per cent will have committed serious offences, 32 per cent will have a conduct disorder and 13 per cent will have a serious mental illness.

16. *Paper 6* highlights the importance of multi-agency, multi-professional involvement in adolescent services, as well as effective preventive measures. It envisages a small core team of forensic specialists offering advice and support in each Region which, in addition to service links, would maintain effective contact with academic departments of forensic psychiatry (the expansion of which has been recommended by the academic development advisory group).

17. It is important that, as far as possible, specialised adolescent services are seen as part of a much wider service embracing a range of agencies and types of provision (health and local authority child care and mental health services, education, Youth Treatment Centres, Special Hospitals, etc). The Children Act now provides the basic framework for services, although the differing provisions of child care and mental health legislation are sometimes an issue. For example, the "mental health" label is understandably thought to be stigmatising, yet the Mental Health Act provides strong safeguards. Utting (1991) *Children in the Public Care* considers these matters in more detail: SN, Annex J.

Young people with learning disabilities or autism

18. Services for children and adolescents with learning disabilities or autism that are relevant to this review are considered in the separate report on learning disabilities. A number of these young people have additional or multiple handicaps. The provisions of the Education Act 1981, which introduced statements of special educational need for children with "learning difficulties" (as defined in section 1(2) of the Act), provide a means of identifying potential problems from an early age. Some fruits of a Department of Health policy review of child and adolescent learning disability services (1988-9) have been subsumed within guidance on the Children Act (*volume 6, op cit*).

Elderly people [Discussion Paper 7]

19. Elderly mentally disordered offenders are rare. Their needs must be viewed mostly in terms of the higher rates of physical and mental ill health of elderly people generally. However, among offenders, there are often problems of social isolation, including homelessness, as a result of which remands to prison are sometimes made when a community option might otherwise have been followed. Similarly, transfers from institutions can be problematic when someone has no active community ties or has lost the ability or will to function independently.

Women [Discussion Paper 8]

20. Figures show that mentally disordered offenders are mostly male. However, women seem to be over-represented in some service sectors (for example, about 20 per cent of Special Hospital patients, compared to only 4 per cent of prisoners). More women than men visit general practitioners with mental health problems and their psychiatric admission rates to hospital are higher.

22. In male-dominated environments, women's needs, including their more personal female needs, are liable to be overlooked. They are sometimes subject to sexual harassment or other demeaning behaviour. *Paper 8* focuses on the need for positive action to counteract these problems and generally to ensure that women receive the care, treatment, accommodation and rehabilitation they need with proper attention to their personal dignity. The staffing and training advisory group has been looking at some of the training issues as well as the need to ensure that staffing policies are attuned to providing the necessary opportunities for patients and staff alike.

OFFICIAL WORKING GROUP ON SERVICES FOR PEOPLE WITH SPECIAL NEEDS

A NOTE ON ACTION TO MEET THE NEEDS OF HOMELESS MENTALLY DISORDERED OFFENDERS

1.   Although, for the purpose of this review, we are considering the needs of homeless mentally disordered offenders, this note also covers some wider issues and action relating to homelessness.

2.   "Homeless" (in this note) refers to people who find themselves on the street, in a squat, in a hostel, in bed and breakfast accommodation, or in prison or hospital awaiting discharge with no family, friends or "home". However, this definition is wider than, for example, that used for the Homeless Mentally Ill Initiative, which is targeted at "rough sleepers".

INTRODUCTION

3.   In London, which has been the focus of several initiatives, homeless mentally ill people appear to fall mainly into three categories:

* people with no previous contact with mental health care services;
* people whose arrangements for continuing care in the community, after discharge, have broken down;
* people who, for whatever reasons, choose to be homeless.

4.   The majority of people with mental health problems (most of whose symptoms are not severe) are supported in some way by families or carers. Resources devoted by local authority social services and housing departments to support this client group are often relatively smaller than those devoted to other groups. Local authorities have been required, since April 1991, to set up inspection units, or comparable arrangements, to undertake the inspection of residential care homes in all sectors (see HMSO (1990) *Community Care in the Next Decade and Beyond,* Chapter 5).

5.   *Voluntary organisations* make a considerable contribution to the provision of housing services for people with mental health problems, especially for those with learning disabilities[1]. Indeed, growth in the voluntary sector in recent years has exceeded that in the public sector. Private mental health provision is also growing rapidly.

INCIDENCE

6.   The Government Statistical Service has stated that, of the 38,460 households officially accepted as homeless during the first quarter of 1992, 4% belonged to the priority need category of "those vulnerable as a result of mental illness or mental handicap" (*Housing Act 1985, section 59(i)*).

7.   Homelessness tends to be concentrated in particular areas with the burdens of cost falling unevenly on authorities. The inner cities are worst hit. For example, of 2703 people identified by the 1991 census as sleeping rough in England and Wales, 1275 were in Greater London.

8.   Most research data on homeless people are collected from settings where males predominate[2]. Almost a third of homeless men have a mental illness but the proportion among homeless women appears to be even higher[3]. Of 49 female users of Government resettlement units who agreed to take part in a study, 41% had a history of mental health problems[2].

9.   A sizeable proportion of mentally disordered offenders also appear to be homeless. For example, of 80 defendants referred to the Bow Street/Marlborough Street court diversion scheme between February and October 1989, only 23 (28%) were settled. Of the rest: 39 (49%) lived on the street, 12 (15%) lived in hostels and 6 (8%) lived in squats. Of these 80 defendants only 4 (5%) had a primary diagnosis of *no* mental disorder[4]. Homeless people are often at greater risk than others of being remanded into custody: see paragraph 28.

CURRENT POLICY

10.   The Government's policy is that people with a mental disorder should have access to all the services they need as locally as possible, from longer-term in-patient care to domiciliary support. For those who can live outside hospital facilities, provision should include adequate housing, day hospitals, day centres, residential care, nursing homes, hostels, sheltered accommodation, *etc*. These issues are considered in the reports of the community and hospital advisory groups, as well as our own report on learning disabilities (mental handicap).

11.   The Government also aims to enhance the role of community sentences and encourage an appropriate use of bail. There are new provisions in the *Criminal Justice Act 1991* for more offenders to serve their sentences in the community. This will increase the number of offenders needing accommodation.

12.   Specific statutory responsibilities include:

    (i) from April 1993 social service authorities must assess individuals' needs for community care services with the aim of ensuring that all care needs are indentified (*National Health Services and Community Care Act 1990, Section 47*). They must notify local housing authorities if it appears that there may be a housing need and invite them to assist in the assessment of that need (*ibid*);

    (ii) local authorities have the primary responsibility for dealing with homelessness. Their main duty is to secure accommodation on a permanent basis for people accepted as homeless, who are in priority need and who are not intentionally homeless (*Housing Act 1985, Part III*). Priority need categories include "those vulnerable as a result of mental illness or mental handicap" (*ibid, Section 59(i)*);

    (iii) district health authorities and local social services authorities, in co-operation with relevant voluntary agencies, must provide after-care services for certain categories of detained patients until they are no longer in need of such services (*Mental Health Act 1983, Section 117*). *Department of Health Circular (90)23/Local Authority Social Services Letter (90)11* requires district health authorities to implement the *care programme approach* for people with mental illness. Social services authorities are required to work with health authorities in introducing this approach and expanding social care services for patients being treated in the community, as resources allow (*Community Care in the Next Decade and Beyond, op cit*).

    (iv) people with mental disorders can, in certain circumstances, be removed from a public place to a "place of safety" for assessment (*Mental Health Act 1983, Section 136*). Some homeless mentally disordered people are identified in this way.

13.   The Government undertook a review of relevant legislation on homelessness. A summary of conclusions (published in November 1989) is at *Appendix I*. One outcome was the publication in 1991 of a *Revised Code of Guidance for Local Authorities* to help them discharge their functions, and secure a better, consistent service for homeless people.

14.   The Department of Health has issued guidance to social services authorities on the planning of community care (*Community Care in the Next Decade and Beyond, op cit*).

15.   A joint Department of the Environment/Department of Health circular to housing authorities, outlining how they would be expected to liaise with social services authorities and contribute to the care planning process after April 1993, is due to be issued shortly. The Housing Corporation is proposing to issue similar guidance to housing associations.

CURRENT GOVERNMENT INITIATIVES

Department of Health

Mental Illness Specific Grant (MISG)

16.   This is available to local authorities to encourage them to improve the social care provided to mentally ill people. 70 per cent is centrally funded. The present review has recommended 100 per cent funding of a proposed additional element for mentally disordered offenders (FN 6.17).

Homeless Mentally Ill Initiative

17.   This initiative seeks to re-introduce mentally ill people who are sleeping rough in central London to mainstream services (CR 3.49; SN 1.16). The programme includes:

    * the funding of specialised short-term hostel places;

    * the establishment of new community-based psychiatric teams providing outreach work with people sleeping rough and support for the short-term hostels;

    * "move-on" accommodation, to be funded by the Housing Corporation, with care costs met by social services authorities. (This is currently the subject of discussions between the various parties to ensure that revenue support for the "move-on" element can be made available).

Single Homeless Young People Initiative

18.   This aims to develop resources in major towns and cities, to encourage and enable young people to remain in their home areas. A total of £3 million over three years is being made available to voluntary organisations for a small number of projects.

Primary Health Care Initiative

19.   This is directed to improving access to primary health services for homeless people and eventually to reintegrating as many homeless people as possible into mainstream services: see *Appendix II*.

Department of the Environment

Rough Sleepers Initiatives (RSI)

20.   In central London, the Government has made £96 million available over three years under the Rough Sleepers Initiative. The RSI is providing some 900 additional hostel bedspaces and, through the Housing Corporation, around 2900 places in more permanent accommodation to which people in hostels can move on. The RSI is also funding voluntary bodies to provide outreach and resettlement work and is funding the Notting Hill Housing Trust to run a pilot "Rent Deposit Fund". The RSI is providing a team of 5 outreach/resettlement workers to work specifically with those sleeping rough in Lincoln's Inn Fields, Holborn with a view to addressing both housing and care needs.

Grants under Section 73 of the Housing Act 1985

21.   Nationally, grants are made under *Section 73 of the Housing Act 1985* to voluntary organisations involved with single homeless people. In 1992/93 grants totalling £6.1 million are supporting nearly 150 projects, offering advice and practical support to homeless people around the country.

City Challenge

22.   The City Challenge competition aims to bring together the work of existing programmes and bodies to tackle the problems of run-down urban areas. Local authorities in partnership with the private sector, local organisations and the community are invited to draw up imaginative and comprehensive programmes specifically designed to regenerate key areas over a five year period. The winning authorities will each receive £37.5 million of public expenditure over five years. Funding for each year of the programme will, however, be dependent upon the stated milestones and objectives in their action plans having been met. Housing was a significant factor in proposals for 1992-93 and local authorities were required to demonstrate a commitment to widening tenure choice and devolving housing mangagement.

Home Office

Probation Accommodation Grants Scheme (PAGS)

23.   The Probation Service Division of the Home Office awards grants, mainly to housing associations providing accommodation for "people leaving penal establishments, referred by the probation service or at risk of offending" (the Housing Corporation's classification of special needs). Those referred include not only people leaving penal care, but also those serving community sentences and defendants remanded on bail.

OTHER INITIATIVES

Housing Corporation

24.   The Housing Corporation's programme includes capital and revenue funding of an additional 3000 special needs units a year.

Inter-Departmental Group on Housing and Community Care

25.   The aim of this group is to review the relationship between community care policy and housing, including any effects on the demand for social rented housing and special needs accommodation, the role of local housing authorities and housing associations in implementing the community care policy, and any financial implications. The group has representatives from

the Departments of the Environment, Health, Social Security, Home, Welsh and Scottish Offices and the Housing Corporation.

Resettlement Units Executive Agency (RA)

26.   The RA is responsible for the management of 15 resettlement units throughout Great Britain, providing 1409 bedspaces. These are direct-access hostels managed by the RA under the *Supplementary Benefits Act 1976, Section 30 and Schedule 5* (as amended by the *Social Security Act 1980)*. Recent surveys of longer-term residents and people admitted to Resettlement Units have shown a high prevalence of health problems including mental disorder. The RA also provides revenue funding for a large number of hostels in London for people "without a settled way of life". These were set up as part of the scheme to replace the Camberwell Resettlement Unit which closed in 1985. In November 1991 the RA was funding 96 projects with 837 bed places in all.

Housing for people from ethnic minorities

27.   There is evidence that black people in particular often face difficulties in finding suitable and good quality housing[5]. Some agencies are addressing this issue and are also identifying an increasing housing need for people with mental illness. One such agency is the Ujima Housing Association, the largest of its kind for black people in the country. It is centred mainly in London and provides 1305 properties for black people. A separate review discussion paper is being published on racial and cultural issues.

PROBLEMS AND POSSIBLE SOLUTIONS

Bail Refused

28.   Homeless mentally ill people charged with petty offences are often refused bail for two reasons:
* lack of community ties
* the need to prepare medical reports.

The latter objection to bail is often raised even when the alleged offence charged does not carry imprisonment as a possible sentence[4]. The growth of court diversion schemes should help to minimise such action, provided that a suitable range of community services is in place to meet individual needs (CR 3.1).

The "revolving door syndrome" and discharge from prison or hospital

29.   An offender's future accommodation should be considered well in advance of discharge from prison (PR 5.36). He or she should be prepared for discharge into the community by learning how to apply for benefits, where to go for assistance, trial visits, etc. Such approaches can help to promote "positive" feelings about the future and offset a prisoner's regarding custodial care as an acceptable option.

30.   In-patients should not be discharged until suitable accommodation and support, and its funding, are agreed. If they are leaving prison at the end of a sentence, however, the situation is immediate and there is a risk that, without proper discharge planning they will be without support. There must be a system to resolve any inter-agency "disputes" quickly: see paragraph 33.

31.   Difficulties could gradually be alleviated by properly structured care programme arrangements (CR 3.14-3.18; PR 5.37-5.38; ST 5.30-5.33; Circular HC(90)23/LASSL(90)11), although, again, this would depend on the availability of a suitable range of accommodation.

Impact of community care legislation on housing options

32.   A number of agencies providing registered care homes dealing with ex-offenders are concerned their clients may fall between or outside Community Care Act "categories" and may not be given a high priority when care costs are transferred from the Department of Social Security to local authorities in April 1993. In addition many of the people in these hostels have had no fixed abode for some years and therefore no obvious local connection.

33.   The Department of Health intends to issue guidance to local authorities to clarify the circumstances in which a person is to be regarded as "ordinarily resident" in a local authority's area and to give advice on resolving problematic cases.

34. There is also a need to ensure that the new funding arrangements do not in fact work to the disadvantage of mentally disordered offenders. This may require concerted action by all the Government Departments and others involved, and possibly the introduction of short-term special arrangements (for example, a specific grant). This is the subject of a recommendation in the main review report (paragraph 8.13).

CONCLUSIONS

35. Although a large number of homeless mentally disordered offenders are in London, there are problems elsewhere, especially in other big cities.

36. Research needs to be undertaken to determine the ways by which people with mental health problems become homeless and also to consider methods that can be used within, for example, the criminal justice system and the community to prevent mentally disordered offenders (and non-offenders) becoming homeless.

37. Services for homeless mentally disordered offenders need to be enhanced. There must be speedy access to accommodation and effective assessment arrangements. Mentally disordered offenders (and other prisoners) ending sentences should be registered with a general medical practice. General practitioners see as many as 1 in 4 of the general population each year for some (mostly mild) form of mental disorder[6].

38. People with mental health problems or learning disabilities should, wherever possible, be able to live in ordinary housing with support services. However, there may also be a need for specialised accommodation. It is important that a wide variety of accommodation is made available to meet a range of needs (CR3.20-3.22). "Hospital hostels" may be suitable for some former long-stay patients[7].

39. Staff working with mentally disordered offenders in a range of agencies should be aware of possible accommodation routes in the area. A local or national database listing beds available in a wide range of accommodation would be helpful.

REFERENCES

(1) Housing: The foundation of community care—National Federation of Housing Associations, 1987.

(2) Scott J. Resettlement units or asylums? Psychiatric Bulletin, Vol 15 No. 12, Abstracts Supplement 4, Dec 1991.

(3) Kingdon D. Homeless and Mentally Ill. Health Trends, Vol 23 No. 2, pp 48, 1991.

(4) Joseph P. L. Mentally disordered homeless offenders—diversion from custody. Health Trends, Vol 22 No. 2, 1990.

(5) Revolving Doors—Report of the Telethon Inquiry into the Relationship between Mental Health, Homelessness and Criminal Justice—NACRO, 1992.

(6) The Health of the Nation (Cm 1523, 1991).

(7) Residential needs for Severely Disabled Psychiatric Patients: the case for Hospital Hostels, HMSO, 1991.

Extract from THE GOVERNMENT'S REVIEW OF THE HOMELESSNESS LEGISLATION, (Department of the Environment, 1989).

SUMMARY OF CONCLUSIONS

In summary, the review of the homelessness legislation has led to the following conclusions:

(1)   the legislation has worked reasonably well and should remain in place as a "long-stop" to help those who through no fault of their own have become homeless;

(2)   the definitions of "homeless" and the "priority need" categories laid down in the legislation continue to be adequate and appropriate to cover the homeless in genuine need;

(3)   local authorities remain the appropriate agencies to make these important decisions, under the Act;

(4)   an amended Code of Guidance is needed to help secure greater consistency between authorities in the discharge of their duties;

(5)   councils must make full use of their existing housing stock. Efficient management should maximise the lettings available to the homeless and to others in need;

(6)   sensitive allocation policies are required, taking account of the priority accorded to the homeless and also other housing needs in the area;

(7)   councils must liaise closely with their local housing associations;

(8)   the voluntary sector contribution to the relief of homelessness is important and should be enhanced;

(9)   good and timely advice can be essential and should be available locally;

(10)   lodgings should be encouraged and the supply of, and access to, such accommodation could be improved in each local area if up-to-date registers of lodgings were available and suitable publicity was mounted;

(11)   mobility can help to relieve housing pressures. The Government are pursuing the setting up of a new single body to promote and enhance mobility across the housing sectors;

(12)   in certain areas, extra help and new arrangements are needed. These "pressure areas" require a committed co-ordinated approach, built on co-operation between central and local government, housing associations and the voluntary sector. The area should benefit from better targeted resources and specific programmes to aid the homeless.

PRIMARY HEALTH CARE FOR HOMELESS PEOPLE

1.   In order to try to meet the needs of this group the Department of Health, in 1986, set up two pilot projects with the intention of providing new models of primary health care. The projects were situated in and managed by the then City and East London and Camden and Islington Family Practitioner Committees. Each multi-disciplinary team included a salaried GP who visited places were homeless people congregated. The team sought where possible to secure the admission of homeless people to GPs lists.

2.   An evaluation study was published by the Policy Studies Institute in June 1989 and was brought to the attention of all health authorities, local authorities and the then Family Practitioner Committees. The evaluation, while recognising some drawbacks in this separate approach to the homeless, concluded that the projects plugged a gap by reaching homeless people not previously seen by a doctor and by supporting hostel wardens and staff.

3.   The two original schemes in London continue, although on a modified basis. In an attempt to integrate them into mainstream services, a single salaried doctor has been replaced by doctors working on a sessional basis. In some cases it has been possible to persuade homeless people first meeting a doctor at a day-centre session subsequently to attend that doctor's surgery.

4.   Following the success of the two pilot projects and a similar scheme in Leeds, special funding arrangements for a further seven schemes had been approved in different parts of the country by late 1991. The FHSAs are responsible for the management of the schemes.

5.   The Department of Health's commitment to the development of these primary health care schemes for homeless people was reaffirmed when, on 9 December 1991, the Secretary of State announced that funding available for recently approved and further schemes would be increased. RHAs were invited to review, with their FHSAs, services for homeless people and to bid for the additional resources. As a result about a dozen new schemes, in areas where it can be demonstrated that there are significant General Medical Services needs which existing arrangements cannot meet, are expected to begin by the end of 1992.

To: Regional Directors of Public Health
Copy: Regional General Managers
District General Managers
District Directors of Public Health
Special Health Authority General Managers
Special Hospitals Service Authority Chief Executive
NHS Trust Chief Executives
Family Health Services Authority General Managers
Directors of Social Services
Directors of Housing
Chief Officers of Probation
Chief Officers of Police
Clerks to the Justices

NHS *Management Executive*

Department of Health
Richmond House
79 Whitehall
London SW1A 2NS
Telephone 071 210 3000

EL(92)24
8 April 1992

Dear Colleague,

Assessment of need for services for mentally disordered offenders and patients with similar needs

1. It is already Government policy that each region needs to develop a range of services for patients with mental illness or learning disabilities who are also offenders, violent or difficult to place for other reasons. The importance of a stable base for such services was emphasised to general managers in EL(90)190 and EL(92)6.

2. The implementation of that policy is currently being examined by a joint Department of Health and Home Office review of health and social services for mentally disordered offenders and others requiring similar services.

3. The review Steering Committee recommended that:

* Regional Health Authorities should, in conjunction with other agencies, ensure that there is a regular assessment of the needs of their residents for secure provision.

4. Regional directors of public health are now asked to assess the need for such provision. The assessments should be produced with the involvement of relevant statutory and voluntary agencies, in particular local authority social services departments, as part of their responsibilities for assessing the care needs of their populations, and criminal justice agencies.

5. The attached annexes contain further explanation (Annex A) and a basic format for responses (Annexes B to E). Assessments should be completed by 29 May 1992, so that the results can inform the work of the review which is due to report in July 1992. Enquiries about this letter should be addressed to Miss C A Miller, Room 113, Wellington House, 133-155 Waterloo Road, London SE1 8UG, Tel: 071-972 4507.

Yours sincerely,

Dr D Walford
Director of Health Care/Medical Director

Dr John Reed
Senior Principal Medical Officer
Chairman, DH/Home Office review

This letter will be cancelled on 31 March 1993

Assessment of need for services for mentally disordered offenders and patients with similar needs

Background

1. It is Government policy[1] that each region needs to develop a comprehensive range of:
    *   accomodation
    *   services

for peoople who are mentally ill or have learning disabilities who are also:
    *   offenders
    *   violent
    *   difficult to place (for other reasons)

so that people needing in-patient treatment within districts or regions do not remain in:
    *   prison
    *   special hospital
    *   the community

2. A joint Department of Health and Home Office review of health and social services for mentally disordered offenders, chaired by Dr John Reed, Senior Principal Medical Officer at the Department of Health, has recommended that:

> Regional health aurthorities should (in conjunction with other relevant agencies) ensure that there is a regular assessment of the needs of their residents for secure provision and of the non-secure hospital needs of mentally disordered offenders, updated annually. We further recommend that this process should start as soon as possible so that regional health authorities produce their first assessment of needs before the end of this review.

> The assessments should include anticipated demand for places for patients from the region for:
> *   Special hospital provision;
> *   Medium secure provision;
> *   Local secure provision;
> *   Local non-secure provision.

The assessment should include consideration, at each level, of 'special needs groups', especially people with learning disabilities (mentally handicapped), people with psychopathic disorder and those in need of long term (over 2 years) treatment and care. It should also take account of the NHS input to community care programmes for mentally disordered offenders.[2]

3. The recommendation has been endorsed by Ministers and this has been announced in Parliament.

Purpose of assessment

4. The purposes of the initial assessment are:
    (a) to enhance local coordinated planning between health and social services and criminal justice agencies;
    (b) to promote local responsibility for special hospitals and regional secure units;
    (c) to begin a move from national norms for secure psychiatric provision[3] to an approach based on the needs of local population and the resources of local agencies;
    (d) To initiate a regular process by which the whole range of services needed for difficult to place and offender patients is assessed and kept under regular review. This should eventually become a joint regular review. This should eventually become a joint agency resposibility. The services covered include assessment and diversion services and general services providing care, treatment and rehabilitation.

Initial scope of assessment

5. The assessment should include the need for secure provision for all mentally disordered people, including those categories of patient at paragraph 2 above. No exclusions should be made on the basis of diagnostic category or expected duration of treatment, though the assessment should identify whether there is a requirement for separate provision for patients with different clinical needs.

6. This initial assessment is limited to the need for secure hospital provision and liaison arrangements with the criminal justice system. Comments are also invited about coordination of assesments with local authorities, given their responsibilities for assessing the care needs of their populations and for ensuring that they are met.

Future scope

7. In future years the assessments will need to become wider, by incorporating other services for difficult to place and offending patients with mental illness, learning disability and personality disorders. Research will also be needed to help determine the scale and nature of the challenge and the form which successful intervention, care and treatment is likely to take.

8. One of the most difficult areas for future assessments will be the need for day and community services, including supervised accommodation such as hostels and sheltered housing, for mentally disordered people who pass through the criminal justice system, but do not require hospital provision. They may find themselves inappropriately imprisoned, detained in hospital or revolving through hospital, prison and the community if suitable provision is not available. If information is already available in some quantified form about the level of met and unmet need for such services this should be submitted as additional information with responses to the main questionnaire.

9. The views of addressees, including copy addressees (who should address any comments through the regional directors of public health), are sought as to how the needs of mentally disordered offenders and others requiring similar services can be assessed in future years such services are the responsibility of a number of agencies, in particular health authorities, local authorities and probation services. Other agencies, especially those in the criminal justice system, also have an interest in ensuring that needs are being adequately assessed and met.

Consultation with other agencies

10. An important factor in the process is the need to consult with other agencies who may be involved in providing services for difficult to place or offender patients. Social services departments in particular have a complementary role in assessing the community care needs of their residents. These include:
  — Special hospitals:
  — District health authorities
  — Family health services authorities/GP fund holders
  — Local authority social services and housing departments
  — Prisons
  — Probation
  — Police
  — Courts
  — Relevant voluntary organisations

Definitions

11. For the purposes of this assessment:
  (a) *Maximum secure provision* means the special hospitals; namely Ashworth, Broadmoor and Rampton;
  (b) *Medium secure provision* means wards or units such as regional security units, usually organised on a regional health authority or sub-regional basis;
  (c) *Local secure provision or low security* means facilities, usuall organised at district health authority level, such as intensive care or special care wards, or units offering care in conditions more secure than an open psychiatric ward with normal staffing levels.
  (d) *Suitable arrangements* for diversion from the criminal justice system means considered adequate by the relevant social services department and health authority as well as by

police and probation authorities or the prisons service as appropriate. If the agencies disagree about the suitability of the arrangements, this should be stated in the response.

Additional information

12. Information about the place of residence of special hospital patients is available from the Special Hospitals Service Authority. A list of the distribution of special hospital patients by district health authority in January 1992 is enclosed for information at Annex F[4]. In future years, the Department will consider whether additional information can be made available centrally about mentally disordered people in prison and in special hospitals. The Directorate of Prison Medical Services is currently compiling a list of names and addresses of prisoners who are thought to be mentally disordered. This will be sent to regional directors of public health as soon as it becomes available (hopefully in time to assist with this exercise).

Format

13. A basic format for reponses is attached as Annexes B-E. If space provided is not adequate then, so long as the question numbers are retained responses can be provided in a different format. Equally, any additional information, for example about liasion arrangements with social services departments, or about services not yet included in the scope of the assessment, may be provided in any suitably concise form.

Time-scale

14. The Steering Committee of the review of health and social services for mentally disordered offenders is due to report to Ministers in about July 1992. In order that the results of this initial needs assessment exercise can inform the work of the review, the exercise needs to be completed by the end of May.

Contacts

15. Special Hospitals:
      Dr J Sylvester (Ashworth)
      Mr M Thomas (Rampton)
      Mrs C Hewington (Broadmoor)

Prison Service:
      Mr J Greenland, Directorate of Prison Medical Services, Room 830, Cleland House, Page Street, London SW1P 4LN.

Department of Health:
      Miss C A Miller, Room 113, Wellington House, 133-155 Waterloo Road, London SE1 8UG.

1. Government response to the second report from the Social Services Committee, 1984-85 session. Cmnd 9673, London HMSO, 1985.

2. Advice on the implementation of the 'care programme approach' was contained in Health Circular (90)23 and Local Authority Social Services Letter (90)11.

3. Health Services Circular (Interim Series) 61 in 1974 required the initial development of 20 secure places per million population. No reference was made to the relative needs of populations in different parts of the country such as rural and urban areas, ensuring they are met. In future years the process is intended to evolve to include the need for non-secure provision for patients diverted from the criminal justice system and mentally disordered people released from prison. In order to ensure a national coverage, responses should relate to Regional Health Authority boundaries on this occasion.

4. Omitted in this report.

Maximum security (special hospitals)

1.   How many patients from the region were in special hospital on 31 March 1992 (please specify which special hospital(s) they were in)?

2.   (a) Are the needs of the region likely to change over the next five years? Yes/No.

If yes, approximately how many beds (it is appreciated that this cannot be a precise figure) are likely to be required on:
   (b)   31 March 1994.

   (c)   31 March 1997.

   (d)   On what basis is this estimate made (e.g. change in local factors, change in other levels of hospital or community services)?

3.   How many of the patients counted in the answer to B.1 are, in the opinion of the responsible medical officer, ready to move to less secure accommodation?

4.   What is the average return travelling time (in quarterdays), assuming a case conference lasts one hour, from individual districts in the region to each of the special hospitals? (this will enable the Department to estimate the time and resource implications of attendance at annual case conferences by local health and social services for each patient from your region in maximum security)

   (a)   Rampton

   (b)   Ashworth

   (c)   Broadmoor

5.   Does the region have a waiting list of residents requiring maximum security (including those who may need long stay provision)? Yes/No

If yes, how many were on the waiting list on 31 March 1992?

6.   Any other comments about maximum secure provision:

Medium security (e.g. regional secure units and equivalents including the independent sector)

1. How many patients from the region were in medium secure provision on 31 March 1992? (including patients in hospitals outside the region)

2. (a) Are the needs of the region likely to change over the next five years? Yes/No.

If yes, approximately how many beds (it is appreciated that this cannot be a precise figure) are likely to be required on:

   (b) 31 March 1994.

   (c) 31 March 1997.

   (d) On what basis is this estimate made (e.g. change in local factors, change in other levels of hospital or community services)?

3. How many of the patients counted in the answer to C.1 are waiting for admission to more secure accommodation?

4. How many of the patients counted in the answer to C.1 are, in the opinion of the responsible medical officer, ready to move to less secure accommodation?

5. What is the average return travelling time (in quarterdays), assuming a case conference lasts one hour, from individual districts in the region to the locations where patients are being treated in conditions of medium security? (this will help the Department to estimate the time and resource implications of attendance at six-monthly case conferences by local health and social services for all patients in medium security).

6. Does the region have a waiting list for patients requiring medium security (including those who may need long stay provision)? Yes/No

If yes, how many were on the waiting list on 31 March 1992?

7. Any other comments about medium secure provision:

Low security (e.g. local special/intensive care or equivalent, including the independent sector)

1.   How many patients from the region were in low security on 31 March 1992? (including patients in hospitals outside the region)

2.   (a) Are the needs of the region likely to change over the next five years? Yes/No

If yes, approximately how many beds (it is appreciated that this cannot be a precise figure) are likely to be required on:

(b)   31 March 1994.

(c)   31 March 1997.

(d)   On what basis is this estimate made (e.g. change in local factors, change in other levels of hospital or community services)?

3.   How many of the patients counted in the answer to D.1 are waiting for admission to more secure accommodation?

4.   How many of the patients counted in the answer to D.1 are, in the opinion of the responsible medical officer, ready to move to less secure accommodation?

5.   What is the average return travelling time (in quarterdays), assuming a case conference lasts one hour, from individual districts in the region to the locations where patients are being treated in conditions of low security? (this will help the Department to estimate the time and resource implications of attendance at monthly and pre-discharge case conferences by local health and social services for all patients in low security).

6.   Does the region have a waiting list of residents requiring access to low security (including those who may need long stay provision)? Yes/No

If yes, how many were on the waiting list on 31 March 1992?

7.   Any other comments about low security:

Criminal justice system

1. How many police stations are there in the region which are registered to detain people overnight?

2. How many of the police stations have a suitable arrangement with health and social services for the screening, assessment and diversion of people who seem to be mentally disordered?

3. Does the region expect to meet the need for suitable arrangements between police stations in the region and health and social services for the screening, assessment and diversion of people who seem to be mentally disordered over the next five years? (other agencies will need to be consulted about their plans to make available elements of these services for which they are responsible)

4. How many magistrates courts are there in the region?

5. How many of the courts have a suitable, multi-disciplinary (health and social services) mental health assessment and diversion scheme to screen, identify and divert mentally disordered defendants?

6. Does the region expect to meet the need for suitable, multi-disciplinary (health and social services) mental health assessment and diversion schemes to screen, identify and divert mentally disordered defendants from courts in the region over the next five years? (other agencies will need to be consulted about their plans to make available elements of these services for which they are responsible)

7. How many prisons are there in the region?

8. How many of the prisons have a suitable multi-disciplinary mental health assessment and diversion scheme to screen, identify and divert mentally disordered offenders?

9. Does the region expect to meet the need for suitable multi-disciplinary mental health assessment and diversion schemes in prisons in the region to screen, identify and divert mentally disordered offenders over the next five years? (other agencies will need to be consulted about their plans to make available elements of these services for which they are responsible)

10. How many of the prisons have suitable multi-disciplinary arrangements for the parole and release into the community of mentally disordered inmates?

11. Does the region expect the need for suitable multi-disciplinary arrangements in prisons in the region for the parole and release into the community of mentally disordered inmates to be met over the next five years? (other agencies will need to be consulted about their plans to make available elements of these services for which the are responsible)

12. Any other comments about liaison with the criminal justice system:

DEPARTMENT OF HEALTH

JOINT HEALTH/SOCIAL SERVICES CIRCULAR

HEALTH AND SOCIAL SERVICES DEVELOPMENT
"CARING FOR PEOPLE"
THE CARE PROGRAMME APPROACH FOR PEOPLE WITH A MENTAL ILLNESS
REFERRED TO THE SPECIALIST PSYCHIATRIC SERVICES

This Circular will be cancelled on 10 September 1995

SUMMARY

This circular:

I. requires district health authorities, the Bethlem and Maudsley Special Health Authority and the Special Hospitals Service Authority to implement the care programme approach envisaged in HC(88)43 (Appendix 4, paragraph 3) for people with a mental illness, including dementia, whatever its cause, referred to the specialist psychiatric services;

II. asks social services authorities to collaborate with health authorities in introducing this approach and, as resources allow, to continue to expand social care services to patients being treated in the community.

It builds on the general circular on hospital discharges (HC(89)5). The Annex to this circular sets out:

I. the policy background to the care programme approach;

II. how the care programme approach works;

and draws attention to some specific matters which will need to be addressed in establishing care programmes.

ACTION

By 1 April 1991 District health authorities and the Bethlem and Maudsley Special Health Authority must have drawn up and implemented, in consultation and agreement with social services authorities, local care programme policies to apply to all in-patients considered for discharge, and all new patients accepted, by the specialist psychiatric services they manage from that date. Where a district health authority purchases psychiatric services from a self-governing trust or elsewhere, the contractual arrangements should require these organisations to have adopted the care programme approach.

By 30 April 1991 Regional health authorities must confirm to the NHS Management Executive (via their Regional Liaison Principal) that all district health authorities in their areas have introduced the care programme approach.

By 30 April 1991 The Bethlem and Maudsley Special Health Authority must confirm (via its Regional Liaison Principal) that it has introduced the care programme approach.

Special Hospitals The requirements set out in this circular also apply to the Special Hospitals under the management of the Special Hospitals Service Authority. The SHSA will need to ensure that action has been taken to provide for the introduction of the care programme approach and should have received confirmation to that effect from each Special Hospital by *30 April 1991*. In particular the SHSA will want to ensure that each patient's care plan enables any transfers to NHS or local authority social services facilities required by particular patients to be identified and arranged in good time.

RESOURCES

1. Health authorities are expected to meet any health service costs arising from the introduction of more systematic *procedures* from existing resources. Introducing the care programme approach places no new requirement to provide *services* on either health or social service authorities.

2. Health authorities will judge what resources they make available for such services. Social services authorities will make similar decisions but will have available specially targetted resources through the new specific grant which is to be used in ways agreed with relevant DHA(s). (Details of the new grant, payable from 1991/2, are set out in HC(90)24/LAC(90)10.

ENQUIRIES

3. Enquiries about this circular should be addressed to Mr G Payne, PHS3, Department of Health, Alexander Fleming House, London SE1 6BY.

This circular may be freely reproduced by those whom it is addressed.

Limited numbers of copies may also be obtained fro the Department of Health Store, Health Publications Unit, No. 2 Site, Manchester Road, Heywood, Lancashire OL10 2PZ, quoting the code and serial number appeariing at the top right-hand corner of the front sheet.

THE CARE PROGRAMME APPROACH FOR PEOPLE WITH A MENTAL ILLNESS REFERRED TO THE SPECIALIST PSYCHIATRIC SERVICES

INTRODUCTION

1.   This Annex sets out:

(a)   the policy background to the care programme approach;

(b)   how the care programme approach works;

and gives guidance on some key issues to be addressed in implementation.

POLICY BACKGROUND

2.   The 1975 White Paper "Better Services for the Mentally Ill" (Cmnd 6233) first set the general policy within which care programmes should be introduced: this general policy has been endorsed by the Government in the 1989 White Paper "Caring for People" (Cm 849), paragraph 7.4. Locally-based hospital and community health services, co-ordinated with services provided by social services authorities, voluntary and private sectors, and carers, can provide better care and treatment for many people with a mental illness than traditional specialist psychiatric hospitals.

3.   Community based services are only an improvement when the patients who would otherwise have been hospital in-patients get satisfactory health care, and, where appropriate, social care. "Caring for People" acknowledged that providing adequate arrangements for the community care and treatment of some patients had proved more difficult and resource intensive than expected. In practice adequate arrangements have not always been achieved.

4.   The care programme approach is being developed to seek to ensure that in future patients treated in the community receive the health and social care they need, by:

(i)   introducing more systematic arrangements for deciding whether a patient referred to the specialist psychiatric services can, in the light of available resources and the views of the patient and, where appropriate, his/her carers, realistically be treated in the community;

(ii)   ensuring proper arrangements are then made, and continue to be made, for the continuing health and social care of those patients who can be treated in the community.

HOW THE CARE PROGRAMME APPROACH WORKS

5.   Individual health authorities, in discussion with relevant social services authorities, will agree the exact form the care programme approach will take locally. All care programmes should, however, include the following key elements:

(i)   systematic arrangements for assessing the health care needs of patients who could, potentially, be treated in the community, and for regularly reviewing the health care needs of those being treated in the community;

(ii)   systematic arrangements, agreed with appropriate social services authorities, for assessing and regularly reviewing what social care such patients need to give them the opportunity of benefitting from treatment in the community;

(iii)   effective systems for ensuring that agreed health and, where necessary, social care services are provided to those patients who can be treated in the community.

6.   It will be for relevant health and social services staff to decide whether the resources available to them can enable acceptable arrangements to be made for treating specific patients in the community. If a patient's minimum needs for treatment in the community—both in terms of continuing health care and any necessary social care—cannot be met, in-patient treatment should be offered or continued, although (except for patients detained under the Mental Health Act) it is for individual patients to decide whether to accept treatment as an in-patient. Health authorities will need to ensure that any reduction in the number of hospital beds does not outpace the development of alternative community services.

IMPLEMENTATION

7. Within the broad framework described it is for health authorities, in discussion with consultant psychiatrists, nurses, social workers and other professional staff, and social services authorities to seek to establish suitable local arrangements, and to see that they are maintained in the context of purchaser/provider arrangements post 1 April 1991.

8. There are some specific issues which all authorities will however need to address in determining their local arrangements. These relate to:
* Inter-professional working;
* Involving patients and carers;
* Keeping in touch with patients and ensuring agreed services are provided;
* the role of key workers.

INTER-PROFESSIONAL WORKING

9. Although all the patients concerned will be patients of a consultant psychiatrist, modern psychiatric practice calls for effective inter-professional collaboration between psychiatrists, nurses, psychologists, occupational therapists and other health service professional staff; social workers employed by social services authorities, and general practitioners and the primary care team, and proper consultation with patients and their carers.

10. Where it is clear to a consultant and professional colleagues that continuing health and/or social care is necessary for a patient whom they propose to treat in the community, there must be proper arrangements for determining whether the services assessed as necessary can, within available resources, be provided. It is essential to obtain the agreement of all professional staff and carers (see paragraphs 12 and 13 below) expected to contribute to a patient's care programme that they are able to participate as planned.

INVOLVING PATIENTS

11. It is important that proper opportunities are provided for patients themselves to take part in discussions about their proposed care programmes, so that they have the chance to discuss different treatment possibilities and agree the programme to be implemented.

INVOLVING CARERS

12. Relatives and other carers often know a great deal about the patient's earlier life, previous interests, abilities and contacts and may have personal experience of the course of his/her illness spanning many years. Wherever consistent with the patient's wishes, professional staff should seek to involve them in the planning and subsequent oversight of community care and treatment.

13. Carers often make a major and valued contribution to the support received by many people with a mental illness being treated in the community. Where a care programme depends on such a contribution, it should be agreed in advance with the carer who should be properly advised both about such aspects of the patient's condition as is necessary for the support to be given, and how to secure professional advice and support, both in emergencies and on a day-to-day basis. In addition, professional staff may be able to offer the carer help in coming to terms with his/her role vis-a-vis the patient.

ARRANGEMENTS FOR KEEPING IN TOUCH WITH PATIENTS AND MAKING SURE THE SERVICES AGREED AS PART OF THE PROGRAMME ARE PROVIDED

14. Once an assessment has been made of the continuing health and social care needs to be met if a patient is to be treated in the community, and all the professional staff expected to contribute to its implementation have agreed that it is realistic for them to make the required contributions, it is necessary to have effective arrangements both for monitoring that the agreed services are, indeed, provided, and for keeping in contact with the patient and drawing attention to his or her condition. This is a narrower concept than that of case management as envisaged in the White Paper "Caring for People" and upon which specific guidance will shortly be given to local authorities. In the Department's view the most effective means of undertaking this work is through named individuals, often called key workers, identified to carry the responsibilities outlined above in respect of individual patients.

15. KEY WORKERS

Where this can be agreed between a health authority and the relevant social services authority, the ideal is for one named person to be appointed as key worker to keep in close contact with the patient and to monitor that the agreed health and social care is given. The key worker can come from any discipline but should be sufficiently experienced to command the confidence of colleagues from other disciplines. When the key worker is unavailable, proper arrangements should be made for an alternative point of contact for the patient and any carer(s).

16.   A particular responsibilty of the key worker is to maintain sufficient contact with the patient to advise professional colleagues of changes in circumstances which might require review and modification of the care programme.

17.   In addition to key worker arrangements, professional staff implementing a care programme may decide that they need a suitable information system as a means of keeping in touch and prompting action. Systems using a micro-computer are available and some relevant information about them is available from Research and Development for Psychiatry, 134 Borough High Street, London SE1 1LB. Tel: 071-403 8790. When establishing such a system, those concerned have a duty to consider how to ensure the proper confidentiality of information about individual patients.

18.   Sometimes patients being treated in the community will decline to co-operate with the agreed care programmes, for example by missing out-patient appointments. An informal patient is free to discharge himself/herself from patient status at any time, but often treatment may be missed due to the effects of the illness itself, and with limited understanding of the likely consequence.

19.   Every reasonable effort should be made to maintain contact with the patient and, where appropriate, his/her carers, to find out what is happening, to seek to sustain the therapeutic relationship and, if this is not possible, to try to ensure that the patient and carer knows how to make contact with his/her key worker or the other professional staff involved. It is particularly important that the patient's general practitioner is kept fully informed of a patient's situation and especially of his or her withdrawal (partial or complete, see paragraph 20 below) from a care programme. The general practitioner will continue to have responsibility for the patient's general medical care if she/he withdraws from the care programme.

20.   Often patients only wish to withdraw from part of a care programme and the programme should be sufficiently flexible to accept such a partial rather than a complete withdrawal. It is important that, within proper limits of confidentiality, social services day care, residential and domiciliary staff (including those from the voluntary and private sectors) are given sufficient information about the situation to enable them to fulfill completely their responsibility of care to the patient. Similarly, relatives and carers should also be kept properly informed.

THE VOLUNTARY SECTOR

Extract from NACRO: "The Resettlement of Mentally Disordered Offenders"

Several national voluntary organisations provide services for people with mental health problems, and some of these also cater for offenders, though primarily those coming out of the hospital system. Mentally disturbed offenders coming from the prison system rather than from hospital care seem to be a forgotten group. Charities working in this field all see the urgent need for more to be done, but also have serious concerns about lack of resources; and some have difficulties or face confusion about who should pay fees, health authorities or social services departments.

Increasingly, charities see the need to collect and share information centrally about what facilities exist. The Mental After Care Association offers care and rehabilitation in a range of supportive environments for adults recovering from all forms of mental illness. It offers both rehabilitation hostels and long-stay homes and co-operates closely with local social services and health authorities, and helps mentally disturbed offenders, primarily coming from hospitals. MACA has set up a computerised database of residential care services for people recovering from mental health problems. It contacted local authority social service departments and voluntary organisations throughout England and Wales for details of homes, hostels and therapeutic communities. It is now planning to extend the database to Scotland and Northern Ireland, and is working on keeping it up-to-date. According to MACA's data bank, there are currently 41 homes which particularly specify that they provide care for offenders with mental health problems, with 412 + beds throughout England and Wales. They are run by a variety of voluntary organisations: Alone in London, St Martin of Tours Housing Association, Carr Gomm Society, Richmond Fellowship, Astra Housing Association, Church Housing Association, St Matthew Society Ltd, Help the Homeless, Salvation Army, United Health Ltd, and some individually owned homes. MACA itself has 20 homes, all of which can offer help to ex-offenders.

Good Practices in Mental Health (GPMH) is a charity which collects and disseminates information about local mental health services which are found to work well both in hospitals and the community, so that others can build on this. It is creating a data bank of information about a wide variety of services in the statutory and voluntary sector. It does not at present have information about services for mentally disordered offenders, but recognises the need for work in this area. GPMH believes that day services could be the 'cornerstone for community-based mental health care in the 1990s'. They can offer therapeutic and rehabilitative services, and long-term help with social and occupational activities. Workers at day centres can help people to rebuild links with families, arrange for housing, and help find work or training opportunities. Although the 1975 report 'Better Services for the Mentally Ill' recommended that 60 places per 100,000 population, or 32,500, be provided in day centres run by local authorities (as opposed to hospital day treatment centres), GPMH finds a considerable shortfall, with only 15,000 places being provided. The House of Commons Select Committee on Social Services noted in 1985 the 'appalling inadequacy of day care facilities for those suffering from, or liable to, recurrence of mental illness'. When it is remembered that the day centres which do exist are not specifically geared to the needs of the mentally ill who are also offenders, it is clear that provision is badly lacking.

Turning Point is a large voluntary organisation providing help for people with drug and alcohol related problems and, since 1985, for the recovering mentally ill. Its Zulu Road project primarily takes patients from Rampton Special Hospital. It offers a therapeutic rehabilitation environment to help residents achieve a degree of normalisation to allow them to live and survive in a community setting. Residents progress from the supportive, communal hostel area to more independent self-contained flats. Help is given with move-on plans and after-care where possible. It also has schemes in Oldham and Worksop which help those with mental health problems, including offenders, referred by hospitals or social services departments. It runs helplines and day centres, primarily for drug and alcohol related problems.

The Richmond Fellowship is concerned with rehabilitation in the field of mental health, and offers help and support to the mentally disturbed to achieve reintegration in society. It offers help to those who have been in prison, as well as those in hospitals, and takes referrals from the probation service and social services as well as from the health service. In the UK it has 60 community facilities, including a day centre and two sheltered workshops, catering for a variety of people. It runs half-way houses, or therapeutic communities, for example, Brunswick Lodge in Reading, which has 14 places, eight of which are for ex-offenders and funded by the Home Office, and which works closely with Berkshire Probation Service. Like other organisations, it feels that facilities for offenders on their own are not as successful as mixed groups.

At the national level, MIND has been actively highlighting the needs of prisoners with mental health problems, having participated in a BMA working party on the health care of remand prisoners, and campaigning with other mental health and penal reform groups to pomote the special and forgotten needs of mentally vulnerable prisoners. MIND has about 200 local associations throughout the country which campaign to improve local provision and also provide services. For example, in the West Midlands, there were in 1988-89 24 affiliated groups, 108 projects including 38 housing projects, 38 day activities, 14 mutual support groups and 13 one-to-one services. However, MIND has not collected at national level information about what local groups are doing to help with after-care of mentally disturbed prisoners, although undoubtedly MIND groups are providing help and support. For example in Liverpool, MIND works jointly with the regional secure unit at Rainhill and the Liverpool Housing Trust in a residential project helping ex-Rainhill patients.

NACRO housing projects provide 750 places for ex-offenders and other single homeless people in a range of hostels and shared housing schemes, with varying levels of support, and working in co-operation with voluntary and statutory agencies. The emphasis is on preparation for independent living. Many of these help mentally disturbed ex-offenders. For example, at the LANCE project in Manchester, which houses 107 ex-offenders and single homeless people, over 40 per cent of residents are being treated for mental illness and 25 per cent are mentally ill ex-offenders. 31 per cent of the mentally ill offenders came to the project on discharge from prison, and 21 per cent on discharge from hospital.

The Effra Trust in the London Borough of Lambeth offers a home for ex-offenders with mental health problems. It works in partnership with a local housing association, and the local housing authority has donated four single flats for those becoming able to live more independently. It offers 17 places, and residents are referred from the probation service, prisons, social services and resettlement units, from all over the country. The Trust works closely with a psychiatric clinic at the Maudesley Hospital, and has good links with local health services. It provides education classes, recreation and an annual holiday.

Lack of resources is a very serious concern for all the charities working in this field. In the words of the Effra Trust:

> 'As for so many charities the future is somewhat uncertain. Although we provide a unique service for some of society's more difficult and unattractive members, we do not easily attract finance or favourable publicity. Nevertheless we are needed. We feel that we deal more successfully with some of our residents than prison or hospital, and are certainly cheaper. We try to help men to become happier and healthier and feel that they are more worthwhile persons. We also hope to help some of them finally step off the treadmill of homelessness, offending, and imprisonment.'

We repeat the thanks expressed to the National Association for the Care and Resettlement of Offenders in the report of the staffing and training group for permission to reproduce this extract.

A NOTE ON LOCAL SECURE PROVISION

1. This annex addresses several aspects of local secure provision and the role of this in relation to other services for mentally disordered offenders or similar patients.

2. There is currently a variety of local secure settings, mainly in locked wards and intensive care areas, but provision is patchy and definitions of what comes under the broad heading of "local security" are problematic. There is, however, a fair measure of professional understanding about what constitute *different levels of security,* and this is considered at paragraphs 16-18.

Hospital advisory group recommendation

3. The Hospital advisory group recommended (HR 5.37) that:

> every district health authority should, in line with existing Government policy, ensure the availability of secure provision for patients with mental illness or learning disabilities. This should include provision for intensive care as well as for those who require long term treatment and/or care.

4. This recommendation has policy and service implications for both general and forensic psychiatry. Many general psychiatric in-patients will need secure care for short periods, as part of their overall management, before returning to an open setting. Other groups with special or differing needs (*eg* children and adolescents, people with a hearing impairment) will also need access to such provision. It is clear that, although more medium secure provision is required (HR 5.36), there also needs to be a range of facilities between this and open local settings in order to meet the assessed needs of the population.

Background

5. At the time of the Glancy Report (1974) there were about 13,000 beds in locked wards in NHS metal illness and mental handicap hospitals. Many of these were not for "difficult to manage" or offender patients. The wards were locked for other reasons: for example to ensure that elderly people with dementia could not wander and inadvertently harm themselves.

6. In 1991, according to RHA returns, there were 639 mental illness beds in some form of local security and 274 such beds for people with learning disabilities. In 1986 the figures were 1,163 and 785 respectively.

7. The reason for the reduction in the number of local secure beds is related to the growth of community care. Although Government policy makes clear that NHS authorities need access to beds in a range of settings (see *Government Response the Social Services Committee* (Cmnd 9674), 1985) a large number of patients with longer-term health and social care needs who used to live in long-stay locked wards in psychiatric hospitals now live in the community. It is equally clear, however, that in many areas insufficient attention has been given to the *range* of services that may be needed for offender and similar patients. As such, some necessary components have largely fallen by the wayside.

Patient mix

8. The overall system of secure provision includes high security (the Special Hospitals), medium security (Regional and some interim secure units, as well as independent hospitals) and lower, or "least", security (local sub-Regional/district provision: *eg* a locked ward). An important feature of secure services is that the mix of offender/non-offender patients changes the lower down the continuum one goes in terms of security. The proportion of non-offenders is highest at the least secure end. Basson and Woodhouse (*Act Psychiat Scand* (1981) 64,132-141) in Edinburgh outline this in their description of a locked/intensive care ward in a general psychiatric hospital. Reasons for admission include absconding and violence, but also suicidal gestures. In terms of general policy, mentally disordered people are not admitted to medium or high security for their own safety alone; they need to be a potential risk to others also (although there is anecdotal evidence to suggest that occasionally such patients have been admitted in lieu of suitable local secure facilities).

Local needs

9.   Basson and Woodhouse found that a 13 bedded ward, covering a population of 600,000, was able to cope with all the acute patients requiring management in a degree of security, 30 per cent of whom were mentally disordered offenders. There was a small number of patients who were chronically disturbed and required a longer stay ward; so a second ward was opened for this group. This gave a total of 25 beds to cover the same catchment area of 600,000. This service is not directly analogous to the district level locked ward in England as Scotland has no equivalent of Regional Secure Units (RSU) and the service described contained patients requiring minimal and medium security.

10.   O'Grady et al (Health Trends (1990), Vol 22 No 1) have described the provision of secure psychiatric services to the city of Leeds (local hospital special care unit, the Yorkshire RSU and the Special Hospitals). They found that the number of RSU beds was short of the target set under the "Glancy" formula for the Regional population: at January 1992 there were 44 staffed and available RSU beds against a target of 71. At District level, Leeds had 16 special care beds or 2.9 per 100,000. The conclusion was that 13 special care beds per 100,000 might be required at district level.

11.   O'Grady compared this finding to a similar study by Wykes et al (Psychological Medicine Monograph, Supplement 2, Part I: 41-55) who attempted to assess the needs for security in one district (Camberwell) of all longer-term mentally ill patients in the community. Wykes found that, at any one time, 18 of the 130,000 population had a need for security or special supervision because they were a serious nuisance or danger to others.

12.   These studies (albeit both in urban areas and each with at least some "inner city" characteristics) point to 32.5 (O'Grady) to 34.6 (Wykes) patients per average district population of 250,000. Extrapolated nationally, the number of patients might be of the order of 6,500. However, such broader estimates are very crude and no substitute for proper assessment of local needs, including those of people with a range of special needs. They are certainly no basis for establishing a "norm": see paragraph 18 below.

Assessment of need

13.   In May 1992 the Department of Health asked Regional Directors of Public Health to carry out an assessment of needs for mentally disordered offenders and others requiring similar services (Executive Letter (92)24: see Annex F of this report). At the conclusion of the review the detailed results were still being assessed, but they already point to a bed requirement above that currently available (certainly closer to the 1986 level). At present such assessments can provide only a rough guide; a database needs to be established, to be built on in the following years.

14.   In another study (soon to be published), O'Grady et al describe a means of assessing unmet need by contacting a large number of sources. This method, which might be replicable elsewhere, helped to inform the Department of Health's assessment questionnaire. The Centre for Research and Information Into Mental Disability at Birmingham University adopted a broadly similar approach to mental impairment in the West Midlands (LD, Annex O). O'Grady found an unmet need for transfer of:

> mentally handicapped [learning disability] patients from Special Hospital to a lower level of security, significant unmet need for medium/long stay secure unit beds and a considerable number of people in the community with significant unmet needs for access to psychiatric services or "asylum" in the community.

15.   Coid (Psychiatric Bulletin (1991) 15, 257-262) underlined the importance of including those in private facilities in any assessment of need. Goldberg found that, in Manchester, only a minority of mentally ill people had "severely challenging behaviour": over the course of a year there were 77 in the whole district or 0.42 per 1,000 of the population at risk (CR 4.4).

Components of security

16. A number of authorities (eg Faulk (1988) Basic Forensic Psychiatry; Snowden (1990) in Bluglass and Bowden (ed), Principles and Practice of Forensic Psychiatry) have described the different components of secure provision with reference especially to medium secure units. For example:

> They are said to provide medium security, by which is meant that they have the capactiy to prevent patients absconding as necesary but at the same time run a treatment programme which will include, as the patients improve, parole outside the clinic. Thus, on such a unit some patients will be virtually as secure as in a special

hospital whilst others will have unescorted freedom of movement into the local community (Faulk, *op cit*).

17. It is not only the locked door (or airlock), unbreakable glass and, in some cases, a small secure external area, which provide security. A high level of staffing is also a factor:

> Security depends also on staff knowing patients well and remaining vigilant. There is no substitute for creating an atmosphere of understanding, sympathy and acceptance. The more acceptable the hospital, the less the patient will strive to abscond (Faulk).

This has been especially so of units for people with learning disabilities visited in the course of this review:

> Units that could loosely be described as "medium secure" (though often relying more on high staffing ratios or extensive grounds than on significant visible security...) (LD 6.8).

18. Fuller (*International Journal of Offender Therapy and Comparative Criminology* 63-77) and Faulk (*op cit*) have described how RSUs have developed in divergent ways. Fuller notes that pertinent variables include "political", structural, human and policy factors. Development has been a "matter for local discretion and initiative". Snowden (*Brit J Psychiat*(1985) 147, 499-507) has described the considerable variation by Region in how quickly services have been set up and the priority given to them. Such variation is reflected also in the wider components of the forensic psychiatric services; factors include differing Regional needs and whether a "parallel" or "integrated" service has been planned. It is likely that there would be diversity also in the development of local secure services.

Current level and pattern of local secure services

19. Local secure facilities have developed sporadically and mainly on local initiatives. Unlike the RSU programme, there has been no direct central funding available. However, in common with some RSUs, progress is often due to a local "product champion". This can have advantages or disadvantages depending on how long that champion is around to provide the impetus.

20. There has been no full assessment to date of the extent of such services throughout the country. Although the needs assessment initiated by the Department of Health will provide some information, it is likely that further research will be needed to act as a spear to development. This should include provision for people with learning disabilities or with other special needs. It is clear that, if all the blocks and gaps in provision within overall services for mentally disordered offenders are to be addressed, adequate services at local level are vital because their availability underpins the possibility for free flow within the whole system.

Design

21. Most locked wards or intensive care wards have been specially converted. However:

> standards of conversion tend to be lower than that for an interim secure unit. Individual bedrooms may be provided and there may be access to a fenced garden. The extent of physical security varies but commonly the ward will be permanently locked and use may be made of unbreakable glass (Faulk, *op cit*).

22. Staffing levels in local units are usually relatively lower than in a medium secure unit, but higher than in a mainstream psychiatric hospital. Usually, the consultant psychiatrist has other duties as well as in the locked ward, and psychologists and other therapists probably need to spend less time per patient than in an RSU.

23. Again, there is very little evaluative research about such services where they exist, nor is much known about the effect of non-availability of such services in some localities. We need further descriptive and evaluative research about current services.

24. There is a great deal of anecdotal evidence to suggest that wards catering for difficult or dangerous patients should not be larger than 15 single bedrooms. Above that size, it becomes very difficult for staff to be aware of what is going on. This relates not only to visual observation of patients but also to having an overall "feel" of the atmosphere and thus being able to respond speedily to increasing tension. There is also the important factor of staff morale; if staff cannot keep a "finger on the pulse" because the ward is too big, frustration levels can rise.

25. Again, smaller units are easier to manage because communication is much easier. This too affects patient management and staff morale. But such factors have to be balanced against financial and other considerations. One disadvantage of some of the smaller medium secure units is that, employing a smaller number of staff than larger units, there is a proportionately greater

effect on clinical capacity if some staff are on sick leave. This can lead to temporary closure of beds. Some have suggested 50 beds as an optimum size, but, again, there is a lack of research to confirm this.

New services

26.   In many cases, the type of design solution for provision of local secure services may be breaking new ground. There may be no suitable precedent to use as a model for a particular situation or set of local circumstances. A number of Department of Health guidance documents are helpful, but are rightly couched in general terms to ensure flexibility of approach locally. For new design solutions to meeting local needs (*eg* possibly siting some small discrete units for people with learning disabilities, adolescents and the chronically mentally ill on one site), there needs to be an in-built evaluative process, as well as a means of communicating to others developing similar services the strengths and weaknesses of a particular approach. Some specific central guidance about these matters would be helpful, perhaps as a follow-up to the current review or through the mental illness task force being established by the Department of Health.

NATIONAL HEALTH SERVICE ACT 1977

Directions to Authorities in Relation to the Exercise of Functions

(NHS Management Executive Letter (91) 45)

The Secretary of State for Health, in exercise of powers conferred by sections 13 and 14 (2) of the National Health Service Act 1977(a), hereby directs as follows:

1. These Directions shall come into force on 1 April 1991.

2. —(1)   In these Directions—

"AIDS" means Acquired Immune Deficiency Syndrome;

"the Functions Regulations" means The National Health Service Functions (Directions to Authorities and Administration Arrangements) Regulations 1991(b);

"HIV" means Human Immunodeficiency Virus;

"in-patient" means a patient who has been admitted to hospital and who spends at least one night in hospital;

"out-patient" means a patient attending a hospital or clinic other than as an in-patient.

(2) Words and expressions in these Directions shall have the same meanings as in the Functions Regulations.

3. Notwithstanding regulation 2(5) of the Functions Regulations (definition of "usually resident"), for the purposes of determining where a person is usually resident for the purpose of regulations 3(1)(a)(i), 5(1)(a)(i) and 7(1)(a)(i) of the Functions Regulations—

(a)   a person who is detained in custody pending trial or pending sentence upon conviction or under a sentence imposed by a court (other than a person whose detention is under the provisions of the Mental Health Act 1983) shall be treated as usually resident either—

(i)   at the address where he was usually resident immediately before the commencement of his detention ("his previous address") or,

(ii)   if his previous address cannot be determined, in the region or district in which he committed the offence for which he is detained or, if he is detained pending trial, the region or district where the offence with which he is charged was committed;

(b)   where a person who is undergoing a course of treatment as an out-patient changes his address during that course of treatment, he shall be treated as usually resident at the address at which he was usually resident when the course of treatment began until—

(i)   three months after the change of address, or

(ii)   the 1 April following the change of address, or

(iii)   the course of treatment is completed

whichever is the sooner;

(c)   where a person who is undergoing a course of treatment as an in-patient changes his address during that course of treatment, he shall be treated as usually resident at the address at which he was usually resident when the course of treatment began until he ceases to be an in-patient.

(d)   subject to sub-paragraphs (e) and (f), where a person who is suffering from mental illness or mental handicap became an in-patient before 1 April 1991 and has remained an in-patient until that date, he shall, until he ceases to be an in-patient, be treated as usually resident either—

(i)   at the address at which he was usually resident before he became an in-patient ("his previous address"), or

(ii)   if his previous address cannot be determined, at the address of the hospital in which he is an in-patient.

(e)   where a person who is suffering from mental handicap became an in-patient before 1 January 1970 and has remained an in-patient until 1 April 1991, he shall be treated as

---

(a) 1977 c. 49.
(b) S.I. 1991/554.
(a) 1983 c. 83.

usually resident in the region or district in which he is present if and so long as he remains an in-patient;

(f) where a person who is suffering from mental illness became an in-patient before 1st January 1971 and has remained an in-patient until 1 April 1991, he shall be treated as usually resident in the region or district in which he is present if and so long as he remains an in-patient.

4.   In addition to the services specified in regulations 3(1)(b)(i) of the Functions Regulations, every Regional Authority shall exercise on behalf of the Secretary of State the function of providing or securing the provision of—

(a) services from clinics to which patients may refer themselves, whether or not they were initially referred by a medical practitioner; and

(b) facilities for testing for and preventing the spread of AIDS and HIV and for treating, counselling and caring for persons with AIDS or infected with HIV,

for the benefit of all persons present in its region

5.   Every Regional Health Authority shall secure, by a direction given by an instrument in writing, that each District Health Authority of which the district is included in its region shall exercise the services specified in paragraph 4 of these Directions for the benefit of persons present in its district.

Signed by authority of the Secretary of State for Health

18 March 1991   *Grade 5 (Assistant Secretary)*

GLOSSARY

This is an enlarged version of the glossary first published with the Steering Committee's *Overview* of October 1991.

Aggressive behaviour. Verbal and/or physical actions or serious intentions that are outside the usually accepted range of harmful or confrontational behaviour, the consequences of which are likely to cause actual damage and/or real distress occurring either recently, persistently or with excessive severity.

Appropriate adult. For the purposes of the Police and Criminal Evidence Act 1984:
   (a) a relative, guardian or some other person responsible for the care or custody of a mentally disordered person;
   (b) someone who has experience of dealing with mentally disordered people but is not a police officer or employed by the police;
   (c) some other responsible adult aged 18 or over who is not a police officer or employed by the police (*PACE Codes of Practice,* Part C, Annex E).

Approved social worker. A local social services authority has a duty under section 114 of the Mental Health Act 1983 to appoint a sufficient number of approved social workers. A social worker who is approved must be experienced and have undertaken special training so that he/she has "appropriate competence in dealing" with mentally disordered people.

Area committees. Local committees, established in the light of the Woolf report (Cm 1456, 1991), which bring together elements of the criminal justice system.

Assessment. Active evaluation of needs. Can apply to individual needs for health or social care, or to the strategic assessment of service needs. See *Needs assessment* and *Risk assessment*.

Butler. 1975 Report of the Committee on Mentally Abnormal Offenders (Cmnd 6244), chaired by the late Lord Butler of Saffron Walden.

Care programme. The "care programme" approach described in Health Circular (90)23/Local Authority Letter (90)11 is designed "to ensure that in future patients treated in the community receive the health and social care they need by:
   (a) introducing more systematic arrangements for deciding whether a patient referred to the specialist psychiatric services can ... realistically be treated in the community;
   (b) ensuring proper arrangements are then made, and continue to be made, for the continuing health and social care of those patients who can be treated in the community". *See paragraphs 4.14-16 of this report.*

Central referral point. A multi-agency referral point for mentally disordered offenders entering or moving between the health and social services (ST 5.40-43).

Challenging Behaviour. Used in respect of people with learning disabilities or other mental disorders who exhibit behavioural disturbance through assaultive, aggressive or destructive behaviour and/or irresponsible conduct.

Circular 66/90. Home Office Circular of 3 September 1990 on provision for mentally disordered offenders.

Clinical. Relating to professional aspects of health care work.

Codes of Practice:
   (a) *Mental Health Act.* Prepared under section 118 of the Mental Health Act 1983. It provides detailed guidance on how the provisions of the Mental Health Act 1983 should be operated.
   (b) *PACE.* Prepared under section 66 of the Police and Criminal Evidence Act 1984. Code C, Annex E summarises provisions relating to mentally disordered people.

Core team. Local multi-professional teams responsible "for ensuring that mentally disordered offenders within a defined area are properly assessed at the "point of entry" (and as necessary thereafter) and then receive, or are referred to those who will provide, the continuing care and treatment they need in the right kind of setting" (CR 3.34). *The assessment panel schemes* that have been established in some areas fulfil a similar, though more limited, function.

Courts. In England and Wales there are 511 magistrates courts and 87 Crown Courts. The powers of magistrates courts to try and to sentence are limited to summary offences only. More serious cases are dealt with by the Crown Court.

Court assessment and diversion schemes. See *Diversion*.

Dangerousness. The difficulty in defining the concept of "dangerousness" was addressed in depth by the Butler Committee (Cmnd 6244, 1975). For its own purposes, the Committee equated it "to a potential for acts which are likely to cause serious physical or lasting psychological harm". But considerable reservations have been expressed about this and, indeed, about most other attemps at definitive statements of what "dangerousness" entails. It is evident that there are widely varying forms and levels of dangerousness as regards both the clinical condition of the individual concerned and the circumstances in which the individual finds himself at any particular time. But the issue of dangerousness, and of the means of assessing and predicting its incidence in individual cases in a consistent and objective way, is central to the work of forensic psychiatry.

Differing needs. See *Special differing needs*.

Difficult to place. Applied to people with a recognised mental disorder which results in their displaying at times unacceptable and/or disturbed behaviour which requires specialised assessment, treatment, rehabilitation and care in a flexible (not permanently) secure environment. Such patients may have previously demonstrated an inability to benefit from provision by the acute psychiatric services as a result of exhibiting behaviour which requires treatment in a more structured and controlled environment over a period greater than that required to deal with an acute psychiatric emergency. Such people often require multi-agency involvement in their care or services which may not always be readily available.

Discontinuance. When the Crown Prosecution Service decides not to proceed with a criminal prosecution.

District Health Authority. One of over 180 statutory bodies in England which are responsible for ensuring the purchase of health care for their resident population.

Diversion. Enabling a mentally disordered offender (or alleged offender) to receive care and treatment from services other than those provided by the criminal justice system. In practice, the term is most often applied when this happens at or just before a court appearance but could also apply to diverting people from police stations or remand prisons. There is a growing number and range of court *assessment and diversion schemes* to identify individual needs and advise as to suitable disposals.

Duty psychiatrist scheme. A type of court assessment and diversion scheme (see *Diversion*).

Emergency application. Admission for assessment in cases of emergency under section IV of the Mental Health Act 1983. In exceptional cases it may be necessary to admit a person for assessment as an emergency without obtaining a second medical recommendation. An emergency application may be made by an approved social worker or by a person's nearest relative. It must state that it is of urgent necessity for the person to be admitted to hospital and detained for assessment, and that compliance with the normal procedures would involve undesirable delay.

Family Health Services Authority. FHSAs are responsible for managing the services provided under the NHS by family doctors, dentists, community pharmacists and ophthalmic opticians. FHSAs are accountable to Regional Health Authorities and work in close collaboration with district health authorities.

Forensic Psychiatry. "*Forensic* means pertaining to, or connected with, or used in courts of law. A forensic psychiatrist's work may be said to start with the preparation of psychiatric reports for the court on the mental state of offenders suspected of having a mental abnormality. The psychiatrist will then be expected to provide or arrange treatment for the mentally [disordered] offender where appropriate. Other psychiatrists and other professionals seeing the sort of patient the forensic psychiatrist is looking after will refer similar patients who may not actually have reached the court or broken the law. In practice all psychiatrists may, at some time or another, have to prepare psychiatric reports on their own patients. Some general psychiatrists have a special interest or responsibility in forensic psychiatry. The term "forensic psychiatry" is used to describe those for whom this is their principal work." (Faulk (1988) *Basic Forensic Psychiatry*).

Glancy. 1974 Report of the Department of Health and Social Security Working Party on Security in NHS Psychiatric Hospitals, chaired by Dr J E Glancy. The *"Glancy target"* for medium secure psychiatric provision was based on an estimate of 20 beds per million population.

Health Care Service for Prisoners. Formerly the Prison Medical Service. This is the part of the prison service responsible for the delivery of health care to prisoners. Following the 1990 Efficiency Scrutiny it will become a "purchaser" rather than a "provider".

High security. See *Security* (*high*).

Intensive care unit. See *Security* (*low*).

"Interim" secure unit. A psychiatric facility established pending the development of a permanent Regional Secure Unit which provides treatment in low to medium security.

Irresponsible. Conduct, behaviour or real intentions that show a serious disregard for the consequences of the actions taken and where the results cause actual damage or real distress either recently or persistently or with excessive severity to self or others.

Learning difficulties. Educational needs requiring special educational provision within the meaning of the Education Act 1981. Distinct from "learning disabilities" (*see below*), but has nevertheless been used by some as a synonym for "mental handicap".

Learning disabilities. Term adopted for "mental handicap". Applies to people with a state of arrested or incomplete development of mind which includes significant disabilities of intelligence and social functioning. Includes *mentally impaired* and *severely mentally impaired* people within the terms of the Mental Health Act 1983. *See* LD, Chapter 2.

Local authority. The council of a county, a metropolitan district or a London borough or the Common Council of the City of London.

Medium secure unit. See *Security (medium)*.

Mental disorder:
> (a) Legal term, pertaining to the Mental Health Act 1983 (section 1(2)):
> *"mental disorder* means mental illness, arrested or incomplete development of mind, psychopathic disorder and any other disorder or disability of mind and "mentally disordered" shall be construed accordingly;
>
> *severe mental impairment* means a state of arrested or incomplete development of mind which includes severe impairment of intelligence and social functioning and is associated with abnormally aggressive or seriously irresponsible conduct on the part of the person concerned and "severely mentally impaired" shall be construed accordingly;
>
> *mental impairment* means a state of arrested or incomplete development of mind (not amounting to severe mental impairment) which includes significant impairment of intelligence and social functioning and is associated with abnormally aggressive conduct on the part of the person concerned and "mentally impaired" shall be construed accordingly;
>
> *psychopathic disorder* means a persistent disorder or disability of mind (whether or not including significant impairment of intelligence) which results in abnormally aggressive or seriously irresponsible conduct on the part of the person concerned".
>
> (b) Also a collective term for the World Health Organisation classification of diseases relating to mental ill health.

Mentally disordered offender. A mentally disordered person who has broken the law. In identifying broad service needs, this term is sometimes loosely used to include mentally disordered people who are alleged to have broken the law.

Mental handicap. See *Learning disabilities*.

Mental Health Act. Mental Health Act 1983.

Mental impairment. See *Mental disorder*.

Mental illness. A disturbance of thought, mood, volition, perception, orientation or memory which impairs judgement or behaviour to a significant extent.

Multi-agency group. In terms of mentally disordered offenders, a local group that brings together elements of the health, social and criminal justice services, and other services as necessary.

Needs
> (a) *"The need for health* is a broad term typically measured by health questions in health surveys, surrogate measures such as deprivation indices, and relative measures such as standardised mortality ratios—all measures which do not easily translate into what

can or should be done to improve health" (NHS Management Executive (1991) *Assessing Health Care Needs*).

    (b)   *"The need for health care* is much more specific. It is dependent on the availability or potential availability of health care and prevention services to respond to the disease or risk factors—and to secure an improvement in health, ie the ability to benefit from effective health, ie the ability to benefit from effective health care or prevention services" (*ibid.*).

    (c)   *Social care needs.* "Social services departments should identify the care needs of the local population taking into account factors such as age distribution, problems associated with living in inner city areas or rural areas, special needs of ethnic minority communities, the number of homeless or transient people likely to need care. From April 1993 plans should identify client groups for whom services are to be arranged, how care needs of individuals will be assessed and how identified service needs will be incorporated into the planning process. The interface between health care and social care is a key area. Concerned authorities should establish shared appreciation of how local needs should be delivered" (*Community Care in the Next Decade and Beyond*).

Needs assessment. A means of defining the nature and level of services required to care for and improve the health of a population (see NHS Management Executive (1991) *Assessing Health care needs*). An initial framework for assessing the service needs of mentally disordered offenders was set out in Management Executive Letter (92)24: *see paragraphs 4.6-7 of this report.*

Outreach services. These are all the activities of agencies relating to a service for mentally disordered offenders which are additional to in-patient assessment, treatment, rehabilitation and after-care of patients. They are community based resources, often to be found in major conurbations and including such developments as out-patient departments, day centres, drop-in centres, sheltered hostels and housing.

PACE. Police and Criminal Evidence Act 1984.

Panel scheme. An extended form of *court assessment and diversion scheme* (see *Core Team* and *Diversion*).

Police. There are 43 police forces in England and Wales. Their main functions in relation to mentally disordered offenders are set out in Home Office Circular 66/90, paragraph 4.

Prisons. There are about 130 prisons in England and Wales grouped into 15 areas. The prison service's main obligations are: to implement the court's decision by keeping the prisoner in custody; to provide a positive regime to help the prisoner make the best use of the time in prison; and to prepare the prisoner for release (see *Custody, Care and Justice,* Cm 1647, paragraphs 1.22-1.28). Wherever possible mentally disordered offenders should receive care and treatment from health and social services rather than in custodial care.

Prison Medical Service. See *Health Care Service for Prisoners.*

Probation Service. There are 55 Probation Service areas in England and Wales which mostly correspond to county boundaries. The special role of the probation service is:
— to provide information to the courts for bail and sentencing decisions;
— to provide information to the Crown Prosecution Service in connection with bail information schemes;
— to provide bail and probation hostels and other accommodation projects for offenders and persons on bail;
— to supervise offenders on probation orders;
— to provide for the throughcare and supervision of offenders released from prison on licence and parole (Home Office Circular 66/90).

Provider. Any person, group of persons, organisations, facilities or units supplying health or social services.

Psychopathic disorder. See *Mental disorder.*

Purchaser/Commissioner. A person or body who buys services, including GP fund holders, health and local authorities.

Reed. Department of Health/Home Office review of services for mentally disordered offenders and others requiring similar services (1991-2), the Steering Committee of which was chaired by Dr John Reed (Senior Principal Medical Officer, DH).

Regional Health Authority. One of 14 statutory bodies in England which are responsible for overseeing the work of a number of District Health Authorities.

Regional Secure Unit. See *Security (medium)*.

Restriction order. An order applied by a Crown Court, in addition to a hospital order under the Mental Health Act 1983, which reserves power to the Home Secretary to restrict leave of absence, and transfer or discharge, and a Mental Health Review Tribunal to discharge or grant leave of absence.

Risk assessment. "*Risk* may be viewed not only in terms of possible physical harm to others or to the patient himself. It may include such eventualities as distress or embarrassment, damage to property, or other offending. It is important that, wherever possible, assessments of risk... are undertaken on a multi-disciplinary basis" (ST 5.36-7).

Screening. An initial examination to determine whether there are any symptoms which could point to mental disorder. Such an indication should lead to a referral for a medical assessment.

Security:
    (a) *Low:* Some local hospitals have wards coping with "difficult" patients which provide a degree of physical security by being locked or having an above average staff ratio. These are sometimes known as "intensive care units".
    (b) *Medium:* Units (including Regional Secure Units) which care for patients who are too difficult or dangerous for local hospitals but who do not require the higher security available at Special Hospitals.
    (c) *High:* Provided in Special Hospitals under the aegis of the Special Hospitals Service Authority. They provide a similar range of therapeutic services as ordinary psychiatric hospitals but in a level of utmost security to enable the treatment of patients detained under the Mental Health Act and who, in the opinion of the Secretary of State, require this because of their dangerousness, violent or criminal propensities. The regimes of care and observation are such that can only be justified when a high level of security is required and a lesser degree of security would not provide a reasonable safeguard to the public.

Serious. Important and demanding consideration.

Severe. Violent, extreme, making great demands upon.

Smith formula. Method used by the Department of Health for calculating enhanced revenue funding for Health Regions that achieve two-thirds of their bed target for medium secure psychiatric provision. (It is named after the official who devised it.)

Social Services Authority. The council of a non-metropolitan county, metropolitan district, London borough, or the Common Council of the City of London.

Social Services Department. The department of the social services authority headed by the Director of Social Services Departments.

Special Hospital. See *Security (high)*.

Special Hospitals Service Authority. The SHSA was established in 1989 to manage the three Special Hospitals: Ashworth in Merseyside, Rampton in Nottinghamshire and Broadmoor in Berkshire. The hospitals were previously managed directly by the Department of Health. They care for patients requiring treatment under conditions of special security: see *Security (high)*.

Special/differing needs. "*Special needs group* is a term of convenience. It serves to identify certain individual patients whose needs are similar and specialised enough to present *special issues* for those purchasing and providing services" (SN 2.1). The term, *differing needs,* is increasingly preferred to "special" needs.

Treatability. When medical treatment is considered likely to alleviate or prevent a deterioration of a person's condition.

Treatment. Professional responses aimed at reducing or removing the signs and symptoms of the mental disorder suffered by the patient and including nursing care, habilitation and rehabilitation.

Trust. A hospital trust is a legal body within the NHS which has the power and responsibility to govern a hospital or group of hospitals.

Woolf. 1991 report (Cm 1456) of an inquiry by Lord Justice Woolf into prison disturbances that occurred in April 1990. A number of its recommendations were adopted in the White Paper, *Custody, Care and Justice* (Cm 1647).

Woolf committees. See *Area committees*.

Printed in the United Kingdom by HMSO
Dd 5128023   C36   11/92   280239 PP